JOURNEY FROM MOUNT RAINIER

JOURNEY
FROM MOUNT RAINIER

A Mother's Chronicle
of Grief and Hope

JUDITH LINGLE RYAN

WESTVIEW PUBLISHING COMPANY, INC.
NASHVILLE, TENNESSEE

ISBN: 0-9776207-5-1

After great pain a formal feeling comes," quoted from *The Poems of Emily Dickinson,* Thomas H. Johnson, ed., Cambridge, MA: The Belknap Press of Harvard University Press, 1951, 1955, 1957.

"Circles," by Richard Murphy, printed in *New Yorker Magazine,* May 17, 1999.

"I Dream of Fish" appeared in an earlier version in *NEWN,* Fall, 2000.

Printed in the United States of America on acid-free paper

Westview Publishing Co., Inc.
P. O. Box 210183
Nashville, Tennessee 37221
www.westviewpublishing.com

In loving memory of

SEAN HUNTER RYAN

(JUNE 4, 1972–AUGUST 12, 1995)

This book is dedicated to parents everywhere

who have lost their children

Two park rangers died [August 12] trying to rescue an injured climber high on Mount Rainier in howling winds and freezing temperatures.

Park Service officials believe the two rangers were within 200 feet of reaching an injured man ...when they fell to their deaths. [The injured climber] was later rescued.

—*Seattle Post-Intelligencer*, AUGUST 14, 1995

ACKNOWLEDGMENTS

I COULD NOT have written this book without the help of many others. My first teachers were Anne Barry, Barbara Bedway, Herb Haddad and Lynn Lauber. I was encouraged to continue by Jim Gorman, Hal Espen, Bruce Barcott, and Sheila Gilooley. Roberta Israeloff deepened my understanding of good writing. Ann Rower's skill in helping me to integrate the themes of writing and grieving is evident on many pages.

I'm grateful to Margaret Wurtele, whose son, Phil Otis, died on Mt. Rainier with Sean. Her book, *Touching the Edge*, was an inspiration, and her feedback on my early manuscript was moving and helpful. My sister, Susan Moeller, brought her journalist's eye to an early draft. At a later stage she put me in the hands of my fine copyeditor, Amy Sharpe.

My thanks to Kathy Krug and Mary Ellen Ellsworth, friends from early in my life, who each gave of their time and talent to read and comment on my manuscript. Thank you as well to Harriet Applewhite and Gerri Karetsky.

Martha Krance graciously put me in the hands of my wonderful book designer, Cindy LaBreacht.

Stefanie Glennon, gifted in intelligence and intuition, has held me steady and insisted that I keep faith in my talent.

Marcy Shover and Dale Singer have each given me extraordinary gifts of patience and affection, as well as excellent editorial advice. I thank Marcy for her ear for language, and Dale for her skills in resource finding. Susanna Willingham offered not only her love, but a writing room in her home when I couldn't work alone.

I am thankful beyond measure for my daughters, Sarah Ryan and Ashley Ryan Gaddis, who are each brave and wise. Their strength and love has allowed me to use my energy for writing. Rob Wieman and Stephen Gaddis, my sons-in-law, have touched me with their tenderness. Steve has been a particular champion of my writing.

My grandchildren—Will and Laurel Gaddis, and Hunter, Eliza and Henry Wieman—have brightened my life and made me laugh out loud.

My husband, Bill, has encouraged me at every stage of this endeavor. He has traveled by my side on the one journey no parent wants to make. I will always be deeply grateful to him for his courage, resilience, and abundant love.

CONTENTS

I
AUGUST
1995

ASHLEY AND I are sitting on the grass outside the back door, flowers strewn around us. The ground is no longer damp with dew, but the morning is still fresh. An occasional motorboat disturbs the glassy surface of the river, and voices of neighborhood children are beginning on the block. The sun is not yet high enough to beat relentlessly and sap what little energy we have. Mingling with the scent of roses and lilies is a faint rotten smell from water we've dumped out of the vases. We're sorting the sturdy blooms from the limp ones, whose petals are luminescent as aging skin, but dry and curling at the edges. After we throw those away, we'll make new arrangements from the blossoms that remain.

Each morning one of my daughters, either Sarah or Ashley, joins me in this task. When we have finished, we carry the flowers back inside and place them carefully around the house and on the screened porch. Satisfied with our work, I take a breath of relief, almost of pleasure. I'm learning that the soft coral pink of a rose petal, or the heavy scent of a lily, or even the taste of a ripe homegrown tomato can pierce just for a moment the cotton batting of my mind, where thoughts and feelings are muffled like sounds in a fog. In that moment I feel still, almost peaceful, free from the pervasive restlessness of raw grief.

This morning Ashley's eyes are dry but puffy. I heard her weeping in the night, in the guest bedroom where she and her husband Steve pushed together the twin beds. Sarah and her fiancé Rob share Sean's big bed on the third floor. Bill and I sleep restlessly in our cherry four-poster, a wedding gift from his parents. Sometimes we lie awake side by side, holding hands, or curl up spoon style, without talking. When we first made love we felt guilty, and we spoke about that a little, but I don't remember what we said. I know that we were shocked by the insistence of our yearnings.

In the early morning only the six of us are here. The kitchen is neat, but unfamiliar, clean platters and bowls belonging to neighbors stacked on the counter, the refrigerator filled with offerings. A few bowls will remain unclaimed five years later. Occasionally, I'll toss a salad in one, and think back to how we were cradled by the kindness of others during this time.

None of us can sleep late, and as we each get up we speak in hushed tones. No one else has arrived yet, but by noon the house will be filling with family and friends. Bill's niece, Kim, who is six months pregnant, sits on our porch each day, knitting a tiny sweater. She appears calm and her quiet presence is a comfort. Her mother, Dale, keeps busy. She sweeps the kitchen, answers the phone, and serves lunch on the porch to whoever is there, digging through cupboards and finding red and green paper napkins left over from the Christmas holidays.

Each morning I try to focus on whatever is most important that day. My thoughts feel fragmented, and it is a struggle to gather them, to wrap my mind around just one task. A phone call to old college friends who lost their son nine years ago. A decision about where to hold a memorial service. An appointment at the funeral home. Sean's body lies in Washington still, in a town called Puyallup, which I've never heard of.

There is a thought that keeps slipping away, the hardest one, the thought about whether we will look at his body. We will bring it back to Nyack, our village on the Hudson River, we will bring him home, but will we have a viewing? That is the term: a viewing. I am afraid. I can't imagine seeing Sean's dead body, seeing how still it is, seeing its scars, but I can't imagine saying no to seeing my own child's body. I carried his body, I gave birth to it, I bathed and tended it, I can't turn my back on it now. But

I have. It's in a morgue, in a freezer. It was autopsied—I don't know what that means or why it was done, and I don't ask. We have arranged for Sean's body to be flown home, but we won't go to the airport. The funeral home will send a car to pick it up—in a body bag? I don't know and I will never ask.

Eight months ago, when Sean returned from college for Christmas, I was so eager to see him that I confused the dates. Bill and I went to meet him at the airport a day early, and I was crestfallen when he didn't get off the plane. We drove back up the New Jersey Turnpike to Nyack, then returned to Newark the next evening to bring him home.

WE HAVE DECIDED to have a wake, since many of our friends and Sean's will want to pay their respects that way. We're planning a memorial service afterward, because Sean's body will be cremated. I think I can tolerate his body being burned more easily than I can tolerate it rotting in the ground. Of course, I cannot tolerate any of it.

Steve and Rob are building a coffin, because it is more unspeakable that Sean should lie in a huge satin-lined lead coffin than in a plain wooden one. Each morning the two young men, who wanted Sean for a brother but are far less certain about each other, go to our friend's workshop to work on the coffin. They wrestle with the pine boards, with their grief, and with each other, and they build a fine coffin, as right for Sean as any coffin could be.

Steve, in an act of immeasurable love, has offered to view Sean's body first, to give Bill and me some idea of what to expect. He knows how frightened we are, but he must be frightened, too. Rob has volunteered to go with Steve. Not yet an official member of our family, he's already carrying his weight. Early on the day of the wake, Bill and I drive with them to the funeral home. After they view Sean's body, Steve says to us, his face pale and crumpled, "It looks like Sean."

Rob adds, tremulously, "But he sure looks dead."

Rob is right. A few hours later I stand briefly by Sean's coffin with Bill. There is no relationship between our son's sleeping, breathing body and his cold, motionless one. I take a long-stemmed flower from a wreath nearby, place it inside the casket, and turn away. Shortly afterward the casket is closed.

Friends and family have gathered on the sidewalk outside the funeral home on this stifling afternoon. As they enter and greet Bill and me, a line forms and I feel as if I'm in a receiving line at a wedding. I retreat to a sofa. Then I feel like an invalid with visitors streaming by, and I hate that feeling, so I stand up again. After two hours the wake is over. In the short car ride home, exhaustion washes over me.

Early that evening I come upstairs at home to find Sarah, Rob and Ashley lying side by side on our bed, still dressed up for the wake, speaking quietly to each other. I think of the nights when our little children ran to our bed for comfort from their nightmares, and I slip quietly past the door.

AT THE MEMORIAL service five days later, I read from A.E. Housman's "To an Athlete Dying Young," beginning with the line, "Shoulder high we bring him home." Standing behind the podium with Bill, my voice is clear, but I'm oddly detached, as if I'm more spectator than participant. I'm wearing a multipatterned, flowing dress that is one of my favorites. In a few years I'll give it away, never having worn it again.

It is late afternoon after the service when we walk home through South Nyack. Others have provided the food and drinks on our lawn, and I realize suddenly that I'm desperately thirsty. A dear friend makes his way through the crowd and brings me a beer.

I go up to bed early, although I can't sleep. Sean's friends from Santa Cruz sing and dance long into the night, and I finally drift off to the sounds of their music. A neighbor has invited them all to his home, where they sleep sprawled throughout his house, some of them spilling into the yard, where they have pitched tents.

EVERYONE MARVELS at how strong we are, how well we are doing. I will know later, if not now, that just as we get up every morning and dress in our familiar clothes, we get up and put on our familiar selves. We do what's expected of us, we stay in our mold, because this is the only way we know not to keel over or run amok. I will understand later, if not now, that our friends and family, who love us very much, are also watching, horrified but spellbound, to understand what they can about themselves should such a tragedy befall them.

I know they're stricken, too, that many of them go home and weep. Often, I can't cry. I'm surprised to discover that when I see tears in someone's eyes or read condolence letters expressing heartbreak, I feel reassured that others are carrying the grief and protest that we're steeling ourselves against. As time goes by their sorrow will ebb, but ours will become more acute. It feels to me as if they're holding it for us, until we're stronger and can take it back.

I have no memory of my dreams. But one morning I wake up suddenly, choking on a sob, and I say in a strangled voice, "He has to come home." Bill reaches for me. I read the helplessness in his face, and instead of sobbing I veer away from my despair. My bladder is aching, so I go to the bathroom, put on my clothes, and go downstairs to boil water for a mug of tea. The warm milky taste of tea helps. Sarah's footsteps on the stairs help, the mindless chat of a news show host on TV helps, cool air blowing through the door of the screened porch helps. I still have not learned how much pain there will be or the myriad ways that I will find to protect myself from pain.

The grief and the veering away from grief will move in lockstep over time. Five years later I will still wake up suddenly, when a dream image of Sean is too vivid, when his presence is too real, and my heart will be pounding, because I'm racing from the despair of impossible longing.

THE FLOW OF VISITORS wanes after the memorial service. Within a few days Sarah and Rob return to their apartment in Manhattan, and Steve flies back to Fort Collins for his first week of graduate school at Colorado State University. Ashley is reluctant to leave.

"I'll stay through the week, Mom. Maybe you and I can shop for the new bathroom."

We spend a morning at Macy's buying towels, a soap dish and good-smelling soaps. Ashley insists on paying.

"Please, Mom. I want to do this."

After lunch we drive to Pier One, but in the parking lot we look at each other, exhausted. This day's supply of energy is used up.

At the airport the next day, as we hug goodbye she bursts into tears.

"Oh Mom," she says, clinging to me, "I didn't want us to be an unlucky family... I wanted us always to be a lucky one."

The plane is boarding. She wipes her eyes, picks up her carry-on bag, and heads for the gate. She looks so sophisticated, tall and willowy in her navy blue silk suit. But I'm remembering the little girl who worried always that something bad would happen, the one whom I could never totally reassure. She straightens her shoulders and disappears into the jetway without looking back.

JUST THREE WEEKS after Sean dies, I turn the key and walk into my waiting room, where the wing chair is covered with fabric of bright-colored fruit and copies of Newsweek are stacked in a basket under the bay window. I cross the room to my psychotherapy office, sit down in my big blue chair and squint slightly from the glare of the sun, which also warms me. When my client arrives, there is alarm in his eyes. He sits down opposite me, pauses, then says, "I heard some terrible news."

"Yes, you did," I respond. We sit for a moment in awkward silence, neither of us knowing what to say next. It occurs to me that I've returned to work for the solace of seeing the familiar faces of my clients, of feeding and watering my African violets, of straightening the brown and beige Oriental rug at my feet, and of sitting in my big blue chair, which is also a rocking chair. I'm here for myself, and I hope that I'm still able to help my clients at least a little bit.

II

AUTUMN
1995

SEPTEMBER 9

As SARAH SLIPS her great-grandmother's handmade satin and lace wedding dress over her head, Maria begins to fasten each button, then kneels beside her to turn up the hem of the wide skirt. Perched on a chair behind Sarah, I can see how the ivory collar of the dress highlights her auburn hair and warms her skin. Her usually pink cheeks are pale.

Sarah and I made this appointment in late July. We didn't tell Maria when we arrived today that in the six weeks since our last meeting Sarah's brother had been killed. It wasn't a decision that we made, but I took the lead in giving Maria a polite, perfunctory answer when she asked how we were. It's too exhausting to talk about with someone we barely know. Maria is an expert in vintage wedding dresses, and this is our only business with her. It's easier to keep our brittle, traumatized selves behind protective shells.

Maybe I'm also afraid that she'd be shocked that we're going ahead with the wedding on October 14, just nine weeks after Sean's death. Sarah picked up the invitations in New York a few days before his memorial service and brought them out to Nyack. I was anxious to see them, but when she opened the box to show me, I felt overwhelmed.

"I can't think about this yet," I said. "Can we talk about it after the service?"

"Sure, Mom," she said gently.

She set them aside and went out to the porch table, where she had spread out photos of Sean. Each day she spent time carefully choosing pictures for a scrapbook, trying to keep herself steady by pouring her love for her brother into it.

Two days after Sean's memorial, we had a family meeting. Sarah spoke up quickly, her voice tense but resolute.

"I want to get married. And I want to go ahead with our wedding and reception in the Berkshires."

I was startled at first by her clarity, but I also admired it. Sarah doesn't express easily her wishes for herself. But she had known Rob since her sophomore year in college, and had wanted to get married for a long time. And Rob had surely sealed his place in our family in the little over two weeks since Sean died. The two of them needed to go forward with their wedding, and not lose that too.

YET I FELT UNEASY about going ahead with it. When my friend, Barbara, called a few days later to suggest a walk, I dressed quickly, eager to share my feelings. Barbara, who is Jewish, was reassuring. She explained that in her faith, weddings aren't postponed after a death, because they represent the beginning of new life. She urged me to put aside any guilt I was feeling.

"You're not dishonoring Sean," she said gently. "He would want Sarah to have her wedding."

"He would want to be here for it!" I said angrily, beginning to cry. "Everything feels crazy and unreal!"

I dug in my pocket for a tissue, and blew my nose fiercely. The wind stinging my cheeks felt bracing, like a slap in the face. If we were going to have a wedding, I had a lot to do.

SARAH STEPS OUT of her wedding dress and begins to pull on her jeans. We're both going through the motions, I think. We don't talk much on the ride home. There are no words for how stunned we are, or how heartsick. The details—her dress, the flowers, the menu—are what we can focus on. She finally found dresses for her bridesmaids at a shop in New York, and Rob picked them up yesterday. She smiles when she describes him roller-blading up Broadway with the dresses flying in a plastic bag behind him. I smile, too, but suddenly I'm enraged at Rob for putting himself in danger. I hold my tongue.

OCTOBER 13

THE TACONIC PARKWAY is bursting with red and yellow leaves on our drive through Connecticut up to the Berkshire Mountains. I can't stop thinking about a walk Sean and I took with his dog, Lady, on another brilliant fall day, a few years ago. The image of the two of us hiking in the woods is so intense that I could burst with sadness. Arriving at the inn shortly before the rehearsal dinner, Bill and I dress, then make our way to the dining hall at Camp Becket. A large group of extended family—Rob's and ours—is already there to greet us. Toward the end of the meal, Sarah stands to make a toast. Beginning with a tribute to Sean, she breaks down within moments, but continues gamely through her tears. Soon we're all weeping. By the end of the toasts I feel drained, wondering how I will get through the square dance to follow.

I can hear the music beginning as we hurry toward the dance hall, where squares are forming. I join one reluctantly. But as the tempo of the music increases, my body responds to the rhythm of the caller's do-si-dos. And as the evening wears on, I fling myself into the release of dancing, beating back waves of sorrow with all the physical energy I can muster.

Shortly before midnight, I fall into bed with Bill, exhausted but unable to sleep. Sarah's wedding day dawns gray and damp. When the first raindrops fall, I run a bath and begin to cry.

SARAH AND ROB are married in a large rambling camp hall, instead of in the open Chapel by the Lake at Camp Becket. Rain beats on the roof as one of Rob's brothers, instead of Sean, escorts me to my seat on a folding chair. When the sweet sound of the French horn signals the beginning of the procession, I stand and turn to watch the bridesmaids' entrance.

Ashley, the honor attendant, is smiling but her eyes betray her sadness. Sarah follows on her father's arm, her face radiant. Bill's pride in his firstborn shines in his eyes, undiminished by the wound he carries. The ceremony is to be performed by Rob's sister and father, both Presbyterian ministers, and, as Beth steps forward I stand unsteadily, grasping Bill's hand. My face feels brittle. Beth begins, "We gather today in sorrow as well as in joy...."

I can't see Sarah's face until the moment when she and Rob turn toward each other to read from Wendell Berry's "The Country of Marriage." Her voice is strong as she begins, "Sometimes our life reminds me/of a forest in which there is a graceful clearing...." As her eyes meet Rob's, a look of such palpable delight passes between them that I feel it as a gift, and I relax and immerse myself in their joy.

As Rob takes his turn to read to Sarah, as they say their vows, as Rob's father pronounces them man and wife, I am filled with gladness, tinged by wonder that I can feel this way. The musicians begin the recessional, and as we follow Sarah and Rob up the aisle and spill out of the hall, I see that there is a break in the rain, and we do not need our umbrellas.

III

JOURNEY
TO MOUNT
RAINIER

S EAN WAS TWENTY-THREE when he died. Well over six
feet tall, he towered over the rest of us. What a triumph,
I used to think, to be the baby of the family and to grow
up to be bigger than everyone else. In college he became
extraordinarily strong, surprising himself and us. He had
grown up late physically, suffering the indignity of watching his best friends outstrip him in height and bulk. But
he had more than caught up. He remained slender, but his
shoulders were broad, and five years of rock climbing had
honed the muscles of his upper body.

In 1995 Sean was spending his second summer as a
climbing ranger on Mount Rainier. On a clear August
afternoon, he and Phil Otis, another young ranger, eagerly
volunteered to carry supplies and equipment to a climber
who was reported injured. They set off shortly after 6 P.M.
and had been climbing for five hours when one of them
slipped. Roped together for safety, they hurtled twelve

hundred feet down a glacier. There were no witnesses to the fall that killed them.

Tomorrow, August 12, a memorial service on the mountain will mark the first anniversary of Sean and Phil's deaths. Our family has hiked in from Sunset Ranger Station for the first of two nights of camping on the mountain that took Sean's life but that he also loved. We've known since the first hours after we learned that Sean had been killed that we would come here to confront this place. In the days before we flew west, I felt a curious mixture of the pleasurable anticipation that I always feel before a trip, and a debilitating dread.

Gray evening light shrouded the mountains as our plane approached Seattle. Bill and I didn't see the peak for the first time until the next day, when we stood on Rainier Vista at the University of Washington. For a year I had traced on maps and newspaper clippings the route that Sean and Phil had taken—their climb, and the trajectory of their fall. I was afraid of my first glimpse of the mountain.

I turned and, unexpectedly, there it was. It seemed to float. On this hazy blue-sky day, it rose above a cottony cloud, its softened contours disguising the craggy mountainside whose ice and rocks could batter young men's bodies, snapping their bones and smashing their vital organs.

The cause of death on Sean's death certificate, dated on our thirty-third wedding anniversary, is "multiple traumatic injuries." We didn't ask for an autopsy report, but we were told by Mike Gauthier, Sean's best friend on the mountain and one of his rescuers, that his neck was broken. I played and replayed their fall in my mind, and I know that Bill did, too, although we rarely spoke about it. Mike told us the only thing that gave us any comfort at all—that there were no signs of life or movement where Sean and Phil lay, no marks in the snow indicating suffering or struggle once they came to rest at the foot of a cliff. Mike told us that Sean looked like himself. I am thankful that someone who loved him carried him off the mountain.

At the site where their fall began, Phil's ice ax remained in the snow. So we know that the scratches in the ice were made by Sean's ax as he made a desperate attempt to self-arrest. Mike told us that on the buildup of slick rime ice he wouldn't have had a chance to halt their plunge. We don't know who slipped, but we know that the rope that bound them guaranteed not their safety but that both would die.

As a toddler Sean loved to climb. I'd forgotten that. I do remember that he was much more physically active than his older sisters. Only a story or song would keep him still. I found some notes, tucked away in a box, that I made before he was two. "He always seems to be on a trajectory upward," I wrote, "onto the washing machine, into the bathroom sink, onto the dining room table." He was introduced to rock climbing on a freshman orientation trip at the University of California at Santa Cruz. I admired him, and was secretly thrilled by his courage and ability, but his climbing unnerved me as well. I told him that I worried. "I'm careful, Mom," he said. "*I* don't want to die."

He went to Mount Rainier for the first time in the summer of 1994 as a volunteer in a summer program in the national parks. Mount Rainier hadn't been his first choice, but he was excited to be chosen at all. On the glaciers he discovered not only the challenge of ice climbing but also the wonder of a brand-new world, high above the tree line, a world of glorious snow fields and rivers of ice. Sean wrote to us that summer describing his first ascent to the summit. The letter was lyrical in its account of the trip. Sean was roped between two more experienced climbers, behind the lead climber Mike, his mentor and idol. Mike's skill and familiarity with the mountain inspired him. Sean wanted to achieve that kind of ease himself. He couldn't wait to go back, and applied for a job the following summer.

He almost didn't get to go. The park was running out of funds. When I saw Sean for the last time, the June weekend of his graduation from UC Santa Cruz, the funding had not been confirmed. He was disappointed, but beginning to adjust to the possibility of staying in California for the summer. A few days later he called Bill and me excitedly to say that the money had come through, and he was on his way to Mount Rainier. We were delighted for him, both of us burying our anxiety and our private hope that mountain climbing would not remain a passion.

Two months later Bill and I flew west to Jackson Hole, Wyoming, setting out Thursday morning, August 10, for five days of backpacking in the wilderness of the Teton Mountains. Late Monday afternoon, August 14, we hiked out of the back country, tired but elated, looking forward to a few more days of camping in the Wind River Range with Ashley and Steve. After that we planned to fly to Seattle, where Sean would meet us and take us to Mount Rainier.

Bill checked us in at the ranger station at Teton National Park, we bought ice cream at the general store, then we climbed into a cab for the half-hour trip to our hotel at Jackson Hole. I remember chatting with the cab driver about President Clinton, who was visiting in the area. When we arrived at the hotel, the desk clerk said, "Do you know that your daughter and her husband are here?" I didn't catch the trepidation in his voice, although Bill told me later that he did. I assumed that Ashley and

Steve had decided to come to meet us in Jackson Hole, instead of at the Wind River trailhead the next day. I took the stairs two at a time and knocked on their door.

Ashley opened it, her eyes wide, and blurted, "I have terrible news. Sean has been killed." I remember spinning around, looking for Bill, who was following me down the hallway. I repeated her words. He slumped against the wall, but stayed on his feet.

Late that night he told me, as we lay sleepless and hollow-eyed in our hotel bed, that he remembered within moments that the flag at the ranger station had been flying at half-staff.

IN THOSE FIRST months after Sean's death, I was agitated, vacillating between thinking and feeling. Thinking was safer. I thought about the fall. Twelve hundred feet. Almost one-quarter of a mile. How far is that, I wondered. I drove along the Palisades Parkway, checking my odometer. I noted when I had gone one-quarter of a mile, and how long it took me, traveling at sixty miles an hour. I needed desperately to believe that it was over before there was too much time for realization, too much time for terror.

I stood on the twelfth floor of a hotel room in Baltimore in November and looked out the window. How high was the ceiling in our room? About ten feet? I calculated about 120 feet to the ground. They fell ten times this far. I figured this out in slow motion, in an intellectual exercise. My emotions were at a distance. I could not let myself imagine how brutal Sean's death had been.

I lived much of this time in a suspended state, cut off not only from horror but also from desire. I couldn't feel my yearning to squeeze Sean's hand, to touch his face, to hear his laughter. The intensity of my love for him was dulled by an enveloping numbness. I couldn't reach down into the deep mother love part of me where I carry my passion for my children. Sometimes I felt that I had lost Sarah and Ashley, too. When I hugged them, a part of me held back. I could not hold them close, and I missed them.

Seven months after Sean's death, I began a journal. "...I almost never remember dreams of Sean," I wrote. "I wake up often at night, but cut off from how I feel.... I woke up yesterday morning with such a clear visual image of him. It was such a relief, ...but I was emotionally detached."

I don't know why I began my chronicle of grief that particular March day, but I must have been trying to penetrate my numbness by putting my sorrow into words. In my second entry, a few days after the first, I wrote, "Sean's absence is relentless, daily, depleting,... I feel that I cannot reach into my own heart except in sadness."

I wondered why I hadn't begun to write sooner. I'd occasionally kept a journal in the past, when I was depressed. Maybe at the beginning my grief seemed too big and awful for words to capture. Or maybe as long as I didn't write about what had happened, it wasn't real. But once I began, I kept at it, determined to recover myself, not become stunted by this loss. Sometimes I cried as I wrote, but I learned that writing calmed me, easing the restless tension that often filled my body.

On our trip to Mount Rainier, I carry a small note-book, although my entries are few. The morning after we arrive in Seattle, I write: "Sean should be here to meet us…. I can see him in my mind's eye—his grin, his pleasure in seeing us." And the next day: "Missing is so different when you are wishing that someone still alive could be with you. You don't feel stabbed."

OUR CAMPSITE IS SHADED, in a circle of trees. We have pitched our tents, and I'm rustling through my backpack for warmer clothes, as the evening air is cool. Sarah and Ashley are talking as they root through our food sack and bring out ingredients for our supper. One of them laughs. My nephew, Michael, is deep in a book, and Steve and Bill are struggling together with the camp stove, which can be pesky. Rob has gone exploring.

Sarah and Ashley spread out food and utensils on a large log near our cooking area. Sarah is twenty-nine and Ashley is twenty-seven, but they look like teenagers. I think about offering to help, but they seem content in their task. My eyes burn a little as I watch them. I am so relieved to feel deeply again how much I cherish my daughters. Tonight I can taste the sweetness of my love for them, my fierce pride in them, and the sharpness of my ache for their grief.

I feel close to them in ways I cannot speak about. I feel deep pleasure in watching them, in seeing their little girl faces in the faces of women now grown. Sarah is speaking, and although I'm not close enough to hear her words, her furrowed brow brings back the earnest five-year-old trying to make herself heard. Ashley begins to chop vegetables for salad, her tongue moving in rhythm with her hands, and I can see the face of the three-year-old learning to cut.

I still revel in their bodies. I can't touch them anymore in all the ways I would like to—I can't squeeze their bottoms, or stroke their faces, or grab them and pull them onto my lap, or tickle them, or tuck them in at night. But I love to look at them. I delight in Ashley's tall, slim body, her full breasts, her shapely but athletic legs, her straight brown hair, which sometimes hides her lovely features. I treasure Sarah's red, wavy hair, and her shorter, curvy, wonderfully shaped body. Her cheeks are a glorious pink, a fresh, clear version of her father's ruddy Irish skin. I feast on them with my eyes.

My reverie is interrupted by a quick, deep breath of longing for Sean. I want to feast on him, too. I search for him in his sisters: I can see his tall lanky body in Ashley's and his chiseled cheekbones in the structure of her face. I can see his strawberry blond hair in Sarah's auburn curls— her fairest strands were his darkest. I can see his dimple and crinkly eyes when Sarah grins.

I search for Sean in the young men who are with us as well. I see his warmth and eagerness to engage in Steve's smile. I can find his gift for boyish comedy in Rob's play-fulness. I see the shape of his rugged features in Michael's face. Michael, two years older than Sean, is my brother's son, and the cousins shared my father's height. As boys they were roommates on innumerable family ski trips, and it was with Michael that Sean first tested himself in the mountains, as they challenged each other to steeper and steeper slopes.

Bill and Steve are about to light the stove, when Rob runs back to the campsite to report that he has found a lookout with a clear view of the peak. It's nearly sunset. We quickly stow the food and hike back with him. At the top of a rise we step onto the lookout, from which the snowscape of the mountain opens before us. I stop, stunned by its terrifying beauty. In the pinks and purples of twilight, I can read the topography of Emmons Glacier, on which Sean and Phil began their ascent, and Winthrop Glacier, down which they tumbled to their deaths. We can see the crevasses, as well as what look like huge snow boulders, then smaller icy peaks and juttings. We barely speak, but I imagine that each of us is mentally traveling the terrain with Sean, trying to figure out where he began, and how far he fell.

THE MEMORIAL SERVICE the next morning is held at another overlook with the same mountain face in view. We gather in a semicircle with Phil's family and friends of the young men. In the brilliant early morning light, the harshness of the slope is clear, but it is no less magnificent. The awful grandeur of the mountain captures me, and I cannot stop gazing at it. A bagpiper approaches slowly from the trail, beginning the service with a haunting dirge. We all speak or read as we wish: poems, remembrances, excerpts from Phil's journals. As Ashley begins her words, two mountain doves rise suddenly from a nearby tree and fly toward the glaciers.

At this service I'm able to weep. I cried very little at the service that we held for Sean a year ago. Shock and disbelief dulled my anguish. But I've had a year to begin to absorb what we have lost. In this setting, among a small informal company of mourners, I'm able to give in to my unspeakable sorrow that Sean, whose promise and possibility seemed to me unbounded, is gone.

When the service is over, I am shivering and hungry, but oddly reassured by the predictability of my body's needs. I'm looking forward to breakfast at Sunrise Ranger Station. We talk briefly with the others over eggs, bagels and hot coffee, but once I am warm and well fed, I'm impatient to begin our hike to Glacier Basin, where our family will spend our second night. We'll set up camp near the site where Sean pitched his tent the first summer he spent on Mount Rainier.

As I hike the path that was so familiar to Sean, I feel a bittersweet illusion of his presence. The otherworldliness of the glaciers overhangs the softer alpine trail, and I can imagine the wonder that he experienced ice climbing. He described it in his letter to Bill and me following his first ascent of the peak: "We walked by 80 foot cliffs of ice that popped out where the ice turned on its brakes. My light reflected the smooth blue surface that dwarfed my presence.... After 45 minutes up top, I struggle with white fingers to get my crampons back on and we head down the mountain.... We jump across the crevasses and pound our knees and thighs, passing the other parties, offer words of encouragement and warning…. The mountain is not friendly to all, not even to most. But it gave me a gift."

I can imagine Sean roaming these lower trails as well, checking to make sure that climbers and campers have proper permits and working to clear trails of rocks and branches. I can hear him chatting with folks, getting to know people, and I can imagine how taken with him those who met him must have been. He didn't always remember his manners, but he was soft-spoken and kind, courteous by nature, with a genuine curiosity about and interest in others.

The hike to Glacier Basin is physically challenging for me, but I'm glad of that. Pushing my body gives me a needed counterpoint to my emotional fatigue. And I'm always enlivened by a new and beautiful landscape. I'm relieved to have met and survived this day and this place, and I feel some solace in getting to know a world that Sean loved. Bill put into words early on something I had not articulated for myself: "I am afraid," he said, "of when there is nothing new." By immersing myself in a world that was also Sean's, I am trying to capture something more of him, something I didn't know before.

Late in the day we reach Glacier Basin: a huge meadow, surrounded by wooded campsites, a rushing river, a graveled slope just below the snowline of the peak looming above the meadow. There's a small lake, where deer will come to drink in a few hours, and there are wild-flowers everywhere. Sean wrote to us from here: "I have been enjoying the evening light, watching the marmots playing around in the meadow that lies in front of my tent, my house for the summer. The snow has all melted out,… unleashing both green grass and beautiful purple, red, white and yellow wildflowers."

Mike Gauthier meets us and shows us Sean's campsite: a small, flat grassy space, just large enough for his tent, next to a log where I envision him sitting to cook, to read, to think, to write. The campsite is tucked away a little from the other campsites in the basin. As sociable as he was, Sean valued time and space to himself. I remember that on the one camping trip I took with him, he would stay up late, after the rest of us had gone to sleep, reading by the light of his head lamp.

THAT TRIP TO THE Tetons, in the summer of 1992, was my first backpacking trip. I was fifty-one, Sean was twenty. He and his father had made a trip to Glacier National Park the year before. Sean wanted me to share their pleasure in camping and hiking. "You can do it, Ma. You'll love it. We'll plan a route that isn't too hard, and I'll carry a lot of your stuff." I did love it, and he did carry a lot of my stuff. We were a group of seven then, too—Bill and I, Sarah,

Sean, and Bill's brother, Tony, and two of his daughters. Sean was stronger than any of us, and could have done our four-day leg in half the time, but he didn't begrudge us our pace. He was growing his hair and a beard and tended toward bizarre combinations of layered clothes. I wasn't sure whether he was making a statement or just didn't care, but I remember thinking that he was a shaggy, mountain version of an overgrown boy. Sometimes he would entertain us all with jokes or stories, but often he'd hike one-on-one with me.

I feel warmed by my memories of that Teton trip, and they almost fool me. My knowledge that today is the anniversary of Sean's death becomes more surreal, and I lose the immediacy of sadness that I was feeling in the morning at the memorial service. Sean must be just ahead, I think, or perhaps around the corner.

That night at our campsite, as darkness falls, Bill reads us a college letter from Sean, in which he wrote about the summer they restored an old motor boat together. At sixteen Sean desperately wanted a newer boat, and he badgered Bill endlessly in an attempt to get his way. Bill stuck to his guns, and insisted that they spend less money and do more work. In the end Sean was terribly proud of the job that he and his father did together. My eyes fill up as I listen.

On this trip, where his presence permeates our stories as well as the landscape, I feel less keenly that Sean is missing. I'm reminded of those first days after his death when, ironically, he lived among us every minute. We held tight to him as if we could restore him through our sheer collective will. We planned his service, arranged beds and transportation for friends of his from all over the country, and listened to his music. But even as we were planning his memorial service, I didn't believe he was dead. I felt as if we were play acting. A year later I still feel suspended in a place between make-believe and truth.

At Glacier Basin I take an early morning walk to Sean's campsite, where I watch deer drink from the lake. The sound of the water rushing down the mountain both exhilarates and calms me. Sean washed and filled his water bottle in this river, perhaps sat as I am doing, looking for wildlife, or just taking in the grandeur of the spot. Sarah is sitting nearby, and I imagine her thinking some of the same things, but we don't speak.

Rob, Steve and Michael begin a climb up a steep, rocky slope in an attempt to reach Camp Schurman, from which ascents of the peak are staged. Bill, Sarah, Ashley and I are left alone and begin a walk together. I turn back, ostensibly to photograph wildflowers in the meadow, but the truth is that I am too sad when we are only four.

The young men return for lunch, and afterward we hike out. At the ranger station we pick up Mike Gauthier, who is hitching a ride into Seattle with us. This van ride is jarring, and it disrupts whatever emotional equilibrium I think I have attained. I sit between Bill and Ashley, and I can see in their faces that they are increasingly upset as well. I have struggled so hard to come to terms with the errors of judgment that were made the night that Sean and Phil died. Although no park ranger except Mike has acknowledged this to us, the Board of Inquiry, which met two months after their deaths, concluded that summer rangers more experienced that Sean and Phil should be hired in the future.

The report notes that Sean and Phil did not protect themselves by anchoring an ice ax when they stopped at the point of their fall. It notes as well that the rescue operations manager that day, under pressure of too little staff, relied on hearsay to establish Sean and Phil's level of experience, their readiness to take full responsibility for a rescue attempt. I know this, and I believe that gradually I have absorbed it. Yet, as Mike begins to recount again what happened that night, at first in response to our questions, but increasingly for himself, I feel assaulted by his words. As he speaks in his rapid-fire intense voice, I feel battered by the details that I both have to know and don't want to know.

Mike carries me to the windswept darkness of the night that Sean died. He confirms that Sean and Phil were let down by a mountain-climbing culture that seduced and then failed them. Sean, who was a veteran of only one other summer, was allowed to lead a rescue. Phil, a newcomer to the mountain, was permitted to accompany him. These two young men were judged capable of deciding that they could safely continue their climb in spite of treacherous ice, howling winds, fifty-pound packs on their backs, Phil's broken crampon, and the pressure of believing that the injured climber could die of exposure. They wanted to go, they begged for the chance, but they misjudged their capabilities. And so did their superiors.

As the van bounces along the highway, I think bitterly of what the chief ranger said to us shortly after their deaths: "Those [rescuers] on the mountain are always in the best position to know whether or not to continue." How absurd, I think, to insist on romanticizing individual choice and responsibility and send two young men to their deaths. Sean and Phil had been climbing for five hours. They were only two hundred feet from the man to whom they were carrying medical supplies, a tent and blankets. They almost made it. This haunts me. But the fact that they were let down by their superiors leaves me with a dull and helpless feeling, and in an empty rage. The fury and despair I feel is different from the emotional storms I have weathered in the past year. I can hardly speak. As Bill and I pick at dinner in Seattle, I can see the desolate look in my eyes reflected in his. Neither of us has wanted to ask the question that our friends asked from the beginning: "What the hell were they doing there?"

I lie awake a good part of the night composing a letter of outrage to the National Park Service. At breakfast I weep furious tears. But my feelings begin to recede as I search for a Laundromat and repack for a kayaking trip in the San Juan Islands. Ashley and I fold shirts and long underwear, Rob and Sarah shop for postcards, Michael goes off to fax a report to his office, and Steve and Bill search for last-minute boating gear. By the time we regroup, reload the van, and take off for Anacortes, my spirits are lifting, and I can hear in their voices that this is true for the others as well.

I still wonder about my rage. Sometimes I think that I have not been angry enough, not only at Sean's superiors, but even at Sean. Occasionally, I feel flashes of anger at him: "Do you know how many of us you took with you when you fell down that mountain?" But he wasn't foolish and he wasn't self-destructive. He made a mistake. My anguish for all that he lost is too great for me to blame him. I just want to gather him up and bring him back to life. The anger I feel at those who allowed him to attempt the rescue is futile and dead-ended. It leaves me with a hollow depression that I can't sustain. The fury could eat away at me, destroy my life, and it would not bring back Sean.

Sometimes my grief overshadows my hope. Sometimes my body aches, swollen with unwept tears, and I'm frightened by the urgency of my longings to have Sean back. But at other times the love and humor amongst us, my immersion in my own life, and the sense of security I feel not only in our family but in our town, among my colleagues, and within the larger community of friends in which we live revives me.

Just as powerful is my own wish to live—and to live a life that contains joy and hope. I've sometimes felt an undercurrent of doubt about that wish. But one night Bill said, musing about his own attempt to make his way through all of this, "I think it would be an indulgence to define my life by Sean's death." That helped me to continue to feel entitled to find satisfaction and pleasure in my own life, even though Sean has lost his.

No one prepared me for how I would live after my child died. No one told me whether it would be okay to turn away sometimes from grieving, to grab life again, or to look for something within myself that I might not have found if he had lived. One year after Sean's death, I don't know what I am looking for, or even that I am looking. But in my journal, three months ago, I wrote: "Reading Carol Buckley's memoir,… I thought about writing a book." And shortly before leaving for Mount Rainier, I sent in my registration for a writing course that begins this fall.

OUR FAMILY ARRIVES midafternoon in the coastal town of Anacortes, where clear air and cool nights infuse late summer gardens with fresh, brilliant color. We spend the night in a small inn, and the next morning we pack our gear and ourselves into sea kayaks. Steve is our leader on a three-day, two-night trip. I have never kayaked before, and I work hard, paddling without stopping for long stretches between our island campsites. At night I am lulled into a surprisingly deep sleep by the soft sounds of the ocean, and by a precarious sense of peace. We have reestablished ourselves as a family in which Sean's ongoing presence remains strong. We have endured the first year. This summer's journey is nearly over.

IV
ASHES

I STEP CAREFULLY into the glare of brilliant sunshine and walk down the path, past the bright tidy flower beds. Don, the funeral director, closes the door behind me. It was unexpectedly difficult to say goodbye to him. I carry with me a blue and white shopping bag containing a maroon felt bag fastened with a drawstring. Inside it is a can with a dent in it, about the size of a large paint can. It's heavy, and labeled simply: "Cremated remains of Sean Hunter Ryan." There is a receipt in the shopping bag, too, which says, "Vandalism fee paid." What does that mean, I wonder. How would you vandalize ashes? Or would you vandalize the body before you burned it? My mind feels unsteady. I remember to look both ways before I cross the street to the parking lot.

I carry with me all that remains of our son's beautiful body: all that is left of that damp, chubby newborn body, that funny rolling-gaited toddler body, that longer, leaner school-age body, that slim, jaunty adolescent body, and that tall, strong grown-up body. A friend said, "I couldn't get over it. He had become a man." He had indeed. At twenty-three he was six foot two. His long ponytail was gone, but a handsome cut framed his newly angular face, calling attention to his fine, high cheekbones.

There is a wonder to our children's developing bodies. It is a miracle every time, the way they grow. I didn't know until Sean died how passionately connected to his body I still was—how much pleasure I took in it. The breathless thrill of watching him run and leap and fling the disc on the Ultimate Frisbee playing field. My eager search for his lope, his grin, as airplane passengers spilled out into the waiting area. The secret satisfaction of watching him cook a stir-fry meal—of absorbing his grace as he moved from spice rack to refrigerator to stove, never still, laughing and talking, bringing home with him an easy pride in his newfound self-sufficiency.

Since Sean died I think often of how I came to know my children through their bodies—their presence was signaled by changes in my own body. By the time I felt them quicken within me, my curiosity about their sex, their features, and their coloring already preoccupied me. After each birth I scrutinized every nook and cranny of my newborn child. My knowledge of my babies evolved within the interplay of touch and response as I nursed, bathed and diapered them.

I keep trying to wrap my mind around this: Sean's body was nothing without his energy, his mind, and his spirit. But how can that be true? I carried him in my womb. I felt secure when I was pregnant, and never feared for the baby's health or safety. After two girls, Bill and I hoped for a boy. We have dramatic photos of his birth— he emerged lusty and feisty, with full cheeks, blond fuzz for hair, and two small flesh wounds on his crown. The obstetrician assured us that this was a rare but benign genetic anomaly. Within a few weeks they had healed completely, leaving keloid scars that would embarrass Sean when he was a teenager.

So many of my memories of Sean are physical. His joyful energy as his sturdy legs propelled him, full speed ahead, across our uncarpeted floor astride his Fisher-Price truck. The surprise on his face, then his uncertain laughter when a wave unexpectedly splashed over us both at the beach. His screams of furious pain when I caught his finger in a nutcracker. "Why did you crack me up, Mommy?" he asked over and over again.

The sound of his voice singing in the shower. He lost all self-consciousness there, even in the year when his voice was cracking, oblivious to the fact that he could be heard throughout the house. The intensity and rhythm he exhibited on his skateboard, pumping with his knees and balancing with his arms as he sped down our block. His growl of obscenities as he reared up in the bedclothes when I woke him up in high school.

I loved having a son. I'd always wanted children of both sexes and felt lucky to have them, but Sean's difference made him more of a wonder. I was amazed that such a fine male body could literally come from me. His body was hard where mine is soft, strong where mine is weak. I admired his long, sinewy legs and his slim tight hips. Early in my journal I wrote: "Sean's maleness allowed me to feel and share and taste—just a little, but so deeply—what it is like to be a boy. He was my only shot at it."

I grew up believing that girls couldn't do the things that boys could do—that they couldn't run as fast, climb as far, be as bad, aim as high. I felt locked into place and didn't have the courage to break out. I counted on Sean to express the part of me that wanted to be a boy, and I lived vicariously through his exploits. He ran and played and skied with a passion that I envied. He yelled and jumped and swore and got up from the dinner table and banged on the piano to get the family's attention. He wasn't afraid to make noise. He played the saxophone, then an electric bass—loud. He insisted on a motorboat. Only in late adolescence did he begin to appreciate the mellow sound of an acoustic bass, or the challenges of sailing. Then, on the cusp of manhood, he was suddenly silent and still.

SEAN HAS BEEN dead for two years. We have finally made a decision to sprinkle his ashes in the Hudson River. It has nagged at me that his ashes were still somewhere in the funeral home, but deciding has been hard. At first we thought of sprinkling them on Mount Rainier, but Bill and I came to feel that Mount Rainier had taken enough of him. We took only a small urn of his ashes with us when we went to Mount Rainier, and gave them to his friend Mike, who wanted to sprinkle them at the summit.

We talked with Sarah and Ashley about burying them, so we would have a gravesite to visit. But little by little a family consensus emerged that sprinkling them in the river felt right. We live on the river, and its presence permeated his life and still permeates ours. We will feel him nearby, yet know, as Sarah said, that the river's currents will carry his ashes to sea, so whenever we are on any seashore we will feel him there as well.

We put off setting a date, but now that we have finally done so, I feel both relief and a much deeper anxiety than I anticipated. It is as if we did not burn his body until I picked up the ashes from the funeral home. And that's the

way it feels. It is we who burned his body, who partici-
pated in its destruction, even though it was broken and
rendered lifeless in his plummet down the glacier.

The body we saw at the wake, the face powdered and
swollen beyond recognition, had little to do with the son
and brother we loved. When he lay there in a sleeping bag,
his face and one hand were exposed, but only two parts of
him were clearly recognizable to me: his hair and his wrist.
I remember his wrist but not his hand, and I don't know
why. I remember how red his hair looked, probably from
the artificial light in the funeral parlor. It was swept back
from his forehead in a strange way, but its texture and his
hairline were familiar. I wanted to touch his hair, but I was
scared. I was afraid that some awful scar from the autopsy
would unexpectedly be revealed. I touched his wrist gingerly. I was afraid of his stillness and his coldness. But the
hair on his wrist still looked alive.

I was both relieved and disappointed that he didn't
look like himself. Maybe only relieved at the time. I was so
afraid of being overwhelmed by my own feelings, of facing
something that would shock me out of my numbness and
unleash the wailing in my soul.

I've always been phobic about injured and dead bodies. I was afraid when the children were growing up that
one of them would get hurt in some terrible way and I

would have to cope—or would fail to cope. When Sean was eight, he and a friend managed to drag their bikes onto the back of a pickup truck parked in our driveway. I was working at my desk near a window, and I looked up to see Sean pedaling rapidly off the truck. Terrified that he had cracked his skull, I raced outside to find him on his feet, tears filling his blue eyes. "I did something very stupid, Mommy," he said, "and I can't move my arm." He wouldn't let me touch it. I cradled him in my lap at the local hospital while the orthopedist gently peeled off his jacket to reveal his wrist askew, a piece of bone piercing the skin. That was unnerving, but not horrifying: no gushing blood, crushed limbs, puncture wounds. I hate vomit, blood and pus, and have no patience even for removing splinters.

So the truth is that I was also relieved not to be there at the foot of the glacier, to take Sean's body in my arms. Mike, his best friend on the mountain, said, "I knew he was dead, but I just wanted to hold him." I don't know, in my heart of hearts, if I would have felt that way. I don't think so. Only later, maybe. I was overtaken one day, months after he died, by a deep wish to have seen his wounds, to know where and how he was hurt. And I was angry because the undertakers insist on making people "pretty"—if unrecognizable—as if we couldn't survive the

truth of a dead body, although we would have had to survive the truth of a critically injured alive body, if he'd
somehow survived. These unexpected feelings emerged, as
if from an underground well, then disappeared again.

I CONTINUE TO struggle with my feelings. I can't bear the
idea of seeing Sean's ashes or holding them in my hand.
After wrestling with my guilt, I give myself a break, deciding that I don't have to be part of everything. Bill, Sarah,
Ashley, Rob and Steve sail without me into the river, and
take turns sprinkling Sean's ashes in the water where he
once sailed and water-skied.

The next morning I'm reluctant to go down to the
shore, fearful that my grief will overcome the peace I've
always found there. That day I feel shaky, unable to get rid
of my focus on the dented can and its contents. Sean's
vitality seems desecrated by his ashes, and the river pol-
luted by their presence.

Yet the Hudson is part of the fabric of my life. For
more than twenty years, I've listened to its sounds, the soft
sounds of a quiet day, and the harsh sounds of a winter
storm, waves crashing over our stone wall, wind howling
as if we lived by the sea. I watch its ever-changing colors—
blue, yellow, green, gray—pale, shimmering silver, or dark
menacing gray. On a hot humid summer day, its blue is

infected by a pale sickly green, and we sit on the porch in the sultry air, sticky and still. There were many days like that after Sean died. Then the heat broke, and the summer breezes returned, and we felt the river's breath again.

The Hudson is grand where we live. It is a wide and open space of water, where the wind is quirky, and the river runs toward the sea, battling the tides, which mix salt with the fresh water flowing from the north. I wonder at the subtle shifts of light and shadow on the river's surface, marvel at its breadth, count on the ebb and flow of its tide. The river is a witness to our life, and to Sean's, and now it carries both his memory and his ashes. As the days go by, I feel a deepening sense that it has been enriched by both, and I allow it to comfort me again.

V

I DREAM
OF FISH

I DREAM OF FISH, vividly colored tropical fish, darting and dancing in the silty gray water of the Hudson. Gazing directly into the underworld of the river through a porthole in my living room, I'm enchanted by their grace and brilliance, but puzzled by their appearance in the Hudson. I want to linger in my dream.

When I wake up, I know immediately that the fish are Sean's heirs, spawned from his ashes sprinkled there last summer. Sean grew up on the river, wading in his sneakers off our lawn, fishing for eels with his dad and his sisters, collecting shells and colored glass, and trying to master the art of skipping pebbles. Once he learned to swim, we took him sailing. A few years later he and a buddy made a raft and were about to put out to sea, when they were collared in time by the friend's father. As a young teenager he learned to water-ski. "Look, Ma!" he would shout as I admired him from shore. He dipped and turned, sometimes his triumph halted by an inglorious crash into the water.

In my dream I felt happy. Awake, I'm immersed again in my sorrow. In this third year after Sean's death, two new lives are beginning in our family. Sarah and Ashley are both pregnant. But today I'm awash in memories of Sean. When he was a youngster, he came home from a school fair with a goldfish, which lived a surprisingly long time. He was so sad when it died. He and I agreed that a watery grave would be suitable, but when Sean heard the flush he ran to the bathroom: "Oh, I wanted to see it one more time."

I am the observer in my dream, as I am in our current family drama. My daughters' babies are safe in their own watery worlds, and I can only witness and admire their mothers' swelling bodies. I wake up with an ache of envy, longing for the child I have lost. But I also feel wonder at my dream, the visual poetry of my unconscious. And I feel an urgency to write it down, to make what I can of its beauty.

When my children were little, I loved to observe them. When they were busy and content, I was often happiest, unburdened by their demands. As they spun their own make-believe dramas, the inventiveness of their play delighted me. But I was also fascinated by what I could not know of them, by the mystery of their private space. I watched them shamelessly, so engrossed were they, and so oblivious to my hunger for them.

Yet, the boundary between us was not fixed. Without my presence they could not have played with such abandon. Their minds unfolded in the safety of my gaze, as mine expanded from the privilege of being their audience. Sometimes it feels that the boundary between Sean and me is no longer permeable. But more than ever he paints my dreams, and he quickens my words.

Sarah, Ashley and Sean swim in the same gene pool, and so do the unborn children. Sean inhabits our memories and our family stories. My children used to beg me at night for "telling stories," tales I told of my own growing up. Our daughters' "telling stories" will always include Sean. I anticipate that our grandchildren will feel at home in our rambling riverfront house, where Sean's bedroom is now the favorite guest room, where photos of him are scattered with all the others, and where his acoustic bass still dominates the family room. The new little ones will be matter-of-fact and curious, and I hope they'll help us to speak of Sean more easily.

From my dream I draw hope, not just illusion. I'm impatient for new life. But my pleasure in anticipation of it is tempered by my urge to hold time at bay, for fear that Sean will spiral further and further into our past. Memories are unreliable and slippery; like dreams, they are timeless but elusive. Sometimes I'm afraid that they'll be eclipsed by the palpable smells, taste and touch of new human beings.

VI

SUDDEN
DEATH

THIS MONTH MARKS the third anniversary of Sean's death. Daily, I feel a rumble of anxiety in my chest, the possibility of panic. At night I sleep fitfully, avoiding my dreams, awakened by the ones I can't escape. I asked Sean once, the morning after an unsettling bedtime story, if he'd had any bad dreams. He thought a moment, then said, "I had one, but I slept right through it." I cannot sleep right through mine.

In the early morning darkness, I wake up suddenly from a nightmare, my heart beating like a child's. In my dream I and another woman, the mother of a high school friend of Sean's, are accosted at night in a parking lot near a wooded area. A young man wants our purses. Rachel is robbed first, and I'm thinking quickly that I could toss my purse into the trees and return for it later, but I'm afraid I'll enrage our attacker. Emerging from sleep, I'm momentarily puzzled. Then I remember that after our grandson's christening in May, I spoke in the churchyard with Rachel:

"How are you doing?" she asked. "How is the family?"

I paused. I never know what to say. "I'm doing well. We're all doing remarkably well. But whenever there's something happy in the family, I can't bear that he isn't here. How can he not be here?" I could hear my voice break.

"I think of you often. I think of Sean often." Her eyes glistened. She loved Sean, who became Robert's close friend when the boys played together in the high school jazz band. An unlikely duo: a skinny, blond white kid, wary of contact sports, and a big, African-American football player.

"How is Robert?"

She sighed. "Still in Texas, still hasn't finished school. I told him that he can come home when he's ready to go back to school. I guess he's not ready yet. Maybe he'll never be ready.... But I don't want you to think I'm complaining." She was suddenly embarrassed.

I knew that she wasn't complaining. I felt her fear that Robert, intellectually as well as musically gifted, would never use those gifts. I felt her worry that she was too hard on him.

In my dream Rachel is robbed first. Perhaps buried in that dream is a wish that my loss paralleled hers: that Sean could come home when he was ready. But my beating heart tells me that in my sleep I'm terrified that what's precious to me will be stolen altogether. I wake up in time to avert disaster, but I still feel scared.

EACH SUMMER a drumbeat of dread in my chest signals the approach of Sean's death date. I wonder if this year I'm feeling for the first time the terror I quashed when Ashley told me that Sean had been killed. I could not have been more unprepared for the news. Our five days in the backcountry of the Tetons had been such a success that I was returning both emotionally and physically exhilarated by it. But on August 13, while Bill and I were savoring the last night of our trek, the South Nyack police were knocking on our door to tell us that Sean was dead. The next morning, while we were eating pancakes cooked over our camp stove, Sean's girlfriend was telephoning Ashley in Fort Collins with the news that her brother had been killed. And while we were hiking out of the wilderness, Ashley was calling my sister and one of Bill's brothers to tell them, and to ask them to spread the news in the family. She was also gathering the courage to tell Bill and me in person. There were no commercial flights to Jackson Hole, so she chartered a plane to fly her and Steve from Fort Collins so they could meet us there.

Ashley and Steve waited for us in the hotel room for an excruciating hour and a half. Meanwhile, Bill and I were coming out of the trailhead, making our way across Jenny Lake by ferry, buying ice cream, and finally traveling by cab back to the hotel. And then, eager to greet them, I was hurrying upstairs. Bill was walking more slowly behind me.

When Ashley opened the door and spilled out the news, I remember saying, "I have to tell Dad." I must have known that if I paused for even a second, I wouldn't be able to give him a message I feared would crush him. I turned and ran to him, telling him as quickly and abruptly as Ashley had told me. I went back to Ashley, wanting to comfort her, and Bill followed.

"How far did they fall?" he asked her.

"You don't want to know."

It was a question I wouldn't have asked, and I wasn't able that day to comprehend the answer. But Bill is an earth scientist and a mathematician, and he had to know. When Ashley said, "Twelve hundred feet," he understood immediately the hopelessness and the horror of Sean's journey down the glacier.

THOSE FIRST HOURS have stayed with me in fragments of memory. I kept repeating to myself like a mantra, "Whatever it was like for Sean, for him it's over now." I must have been trying to beat back the horror of imagining his pain and terror.

I felt dazed but restless at the same time. I barely cried, and I didn't scream or rage. It was a struggle to form

thoughts, as Bill and I turned to the task of making calls—
to the chief ranger at Mount Rainier, who told us little
more than Ashley and Steve had reported, then to Bill's
mother and brothers, and to my brother and sister. Sarah
and Rob were visiting friends in New England, but no one
knew exactly where. Desperate to reach them before Sean's
name was released to the media, I racked my brain, finally
coming up with the name of Rob's closest college friend. I
called information in Williamstown, Massachusetts,
insisting that the operator search under four different
spellings. It felt like a tiny triumph to find the number,
but there was no answer to my call.

Distracted by how dirty I was after five days in the
wilderness—my scalp itching, my body gritty all over—I
was also ashamed of what seemed like a trivial preoccupation. Finally, I couldn't stand it anymore. I retreated to a
hot shower, lathering and scrubbing as if I could scour
away the horror of what had happened.

After a sleepless night in Jackson Hole, the four of us
boarded the small plane back to Fort Collins, flying over
Wyoming's Wind River Range. Bill and Sean had back-
packed there three years before. From fifteen thousand feet
Bill wept as he pointed out the lakes and valleys marking
their campsites. In Fort Collins Ashley and Steve packed
for the trip back to Nyack, and we returned to the local

airport. While we were in the air, Steve's mother finally tracked down Sarah and Rob. A close friend of Rob's family, with whom they were staying in Boston, told Sarah that her brother was dead.

THREE YEARS LATER, as I try to rein in my nightmares, I think about how we were humiliated by fate, caught trusting in our good fortune, brought to our knees at a moment of pride in our own successful mountain trek.

There was no warning. No phone call in the middle of the night, when one's heart beats fast at the sound of the first ring. No policeman at the front door. Only dear Ashley, terrified of what the news would do to us, but desperate to share her burden, blurting it out. I wonder now if in the droplet of time before she said the word "killed," I grasped a wild, searching hope for something—anything—other than death. The news came so fast, and from such an unexpected source, that my anxiety was short-circuited. There wasn't even a moment to bargain with fate, to plead with doctors, to comfort Sean, or to prepare myself.

It is this August, three years later, that I am tasting my panic in frequent nightmares of danger and escape. Like a little girl playing with action figures, I try to master the trauma by disguising the players and revising the ending. Sean rarely appears directly in these dreams. If I recognize him, and he escapes death, I must relive the horror of the truth when I wake up.

WHAT IS THE TERROR that accompanies the shock and sorrow of a sudden death? Because there is no warning, there is no time to prepare. The news that Sean had been killed assaulted my identity, and it felt like an attack on my mind. I was stunned and frightened. Not only could I not imagine the emptiness and yearning of living without Sean, but I also felt panicked by my experience of standing face-to-face with paradoxical and irreconcilable truths. My belief that I had a healthy, vibrant son was starkly contradicted by news that his body was grievously broken and that he was dead.

I held these two truths side by side, like two snapshots, trying to make sense of the contradiction. My mind was full of assumptions that would have to come tumbling down—I'm the mother of a living son, I'm the mother of three living children, our family is whole, our family is lucky, Sean has a full life before him, I'll be kayaking with him in the San Juan Islands next week, he'll be coming to New York for Sarah's wedding in October.

I couldn't grasp my own reality. This was different from the fear that I couldn't withstand the anguish of missing Sean, or that Bill and our daughters would be crippled by their sorrow. I was afraid of losing my mind. I couldn't reassemble the pieces of the shattered picture on which my sense of self depended. What if, like Humpty Dumpty, I could never be put together again?

So I retreated to Emily Dickinson's "formal feeling," where "feet mechanically go round," and "[Nerves] sit ceremonious, like Tombs." Perhaps the numbness not only anesthetized me, but allowed me to hold the contradictions until I could begin to comprehend our new reality, and re-create the illusion of control by which we live.

Belief in Sean's absence grew slowly. Days of tears and fatigue alternated with days when I felt an unnatural sense of well-being, giving me respite from the harsh task of re-creating in my mind our family map. Slowly, contradiction evolved into paradox. We're still a nuclear family of five, even though we're only four. I'm still the mother of a son, even though he is not alive. "How many children do you have?" If I choose to say "two" to the hapless questioner, the answer is also "three."

THE SUMMER THAT Sean died was the summer of a terrible drought in the Northeast. The lack of rain delivered a final blow to a hillside of old rhododendrons on our property, overlooking the Hudson River. The following spring we cut back the stricken bushes, planted new shrubs and, on

Sean's birthday in early June, a flowering crabapple tree. That August, as we approached the first anniversary of Sean's death, I dreamed that there was a terrible wind and rainstorm, with waves crashing over our seawall, engulfing the vegetation. I was afraid that all we had planted would be uprooted and destroyed, but in my dream the new landscape held.

THAT FIRST YEAR my dream was reassuring. Why do I feel my terror now? Am I afraid that my new inner landscape will not, after all, hold? I don't think so. Three years later I feel more certain that I can hold the conundrum of Sean's presence and absence, that I have regained a sturdy sense of my family and of myself.

My sense of sturdiness is strengthened by writing. I rarely write in my journal anymore, because I'm concentrating on crafting essays. They help me to untangle the knot of feelings that make up my grief. I awake from a dream, and I begin immediately to write in my head—not just to record the dream but to make a story of its meaning. Sometimes I scribble a paragraph on paper, sometimes only a phrase. Sometimes I go to my study and write something more.

What I write this August is fragmentary. As I approach Sean's death date, I'm too restless, the pain is too inchoate for me to capture it in paragraphs or in a coherent tale, except in my nightmares. But I know now that once August has passed, I'll be able to wrestle this month's terror—which is really the terror of 1995—onto the page. And that in time I will create a story—this story—of what is happening to me. With increasing faith in my craft, I can dare to slip into the feelings of those first moments, and the minutes and hours that followed. I can dare to experience my fear of cracking, more secure in the conviction that I have found a way to put myself back together again.

VII

REMEMBERING SEAN

S EAN IS RUNNING, arm outstretched, mortarboard in hand, running to catch up with us, his graduation gown flapping at his knees. Ashley turned and caught him on film. Now, almost four years later and two months after Christmas, I'm holding framed photos of my new grandsons. Looking for a place to display them, I come upon this simple snapshot of Sean, which now haunts me. He will never catch up.

In the first months after Sean died, I tried to stop, too. I wished desperately to hold time still, to keep the distance between us and him from widening. I could pretend. In spite of Sarah and Rob's wedding, Ashley's master's degree graduation, then Sarah's, I tried to run in place. None of us had changed physically in ways that were easily noticeable. We were a family of adults, and I could pretend. An occasional new family picture appeared in the living room or dining room, slipped in among the others. Sometimes I found one of Sean that I loved and added it, too.

The arrival of Will and Hunter disrupted my pace, exposed the pretense. Grown-ups evolve slowly into their older selves. But babies unfold rapidly, in kaleidoscopic fashion. Time speeds up in their presence—they seem to change day by day, even hour by hour. Pictures of brand-new baby boys have proliferated. Like vases of fresh flowers, they gladden the house, and I want them everywhere. But there's no room for more. I have to weed out.

How will I do this? The photos throughout our home mark our evolution as a family, and the metamorphosis of each of us as time goes on. I like being surrounded by them. I want Will and Hunter to surround me, and Ashley, Steve, Sarah and Rob in their incarnations as new parents. But what about Sean? Inevitably, he will be outpaced by the rest of us. He won't keep up.

On the upright piano in the dining room is a crowded, disorderly procession of family members. It includes two baby pictures in a tiny double frame, one of Sarah and the other of Sean, their grins and their red-blond hair almost indistinguishable. One of my favorite photos is of Sarah, Ashley and Sean smiling into a preset lens on their trip to Europe the year Ashley graduated from college. And I am struck by how handsome Bill is, relaxed and dimpled, standing on the deck of a research ship with Seattle's needle in the background. This was fifteen years before Seattle became linked for us with tragedy.

Photos of Sean outnumber the others. At fifteen he's looking cool in Moscow, jockeying for position with other members of the Nyack High School Jazz Band. In a snapshot taken at college, he's slouching casually against his truck with his good friend, JP. In 1991 he's fly-fishing in Glacier National Park, the sweetness of his smile under his broad-brimmed hat uncompromised by his pleasure in being photographed. In a photo taken one month before he died, Sean's face is equal parts concentration and exhilaration, as he scales the icy wall of a crevasse on Mount Rainier. The red stubble on his face and silver loop in his ear glisten in the sunlight. His large hands, grasping the rope, are taut and strong. Unexpectedly, I'm flooded by their familiarity, and I want to grasp them, to feel their warmth.

There are no new pictures of Sean. Do I keep recycling the old ones, moving them from room to room? Do I put them in drawers or boxes, waiting to be organized? Organized how? A memorial album? A wall of photos that becomes a shrine? However I do it, will they become like freeze-dried roses, beautiful but without the vitality of up-to-date pictures that seem to leap from the frame? As the new babies crowd onto the piano and into my heart, how will I keep Sean alive?

NOT LONG AGO, I dreamed of Sean as a preschooler, maybe three or four years old. He was waking up, warm and adorable, and I picked him up and held him close. The delicious pleasure of him was palpable, but so was my sense of foreboding. I could not bear to immerse myself in the smell and feel of him, in the sweetness of his voice, because even in my dream I knew that I would lose him. I woke up on the verge of a sob.

Photographs can be just as heart wrenching. Since the first weeks after Sean's death, I've found myself drawn to them, then veering away, reluctant to let them bring back the sound and movement and touch of my son.

Occasionally, I ask myself a guilty question that I voice to no one: what if we hadn't had a third child? Might it have been better to escape the devastation of losing Sean? If I hadn't experienced the joys and tribulations of raising him, I wouldn't know what I had missed and I wouldn't be suffering so. The hope of others—indeed my own hope—that memories would comfort me, has sometimes seemed vain and foolish. How can memories of my own child, whom I can no longer hold, bring anything but the despairing ache of wanting him?

Can I learn to bear remembering? From the beginning I've struggled with this question. And can I recover the parts of me that seem to have died with Sean? The parts of me that are still mother to a son. The parts of me that adored him, flirted with him, hated him, fought with him, admired him and envied him. The parts of me that were stronger and happier because I had a son. The notion that new parts of me might emerge—new ways of remembering Sean—was at first inconceivable.

IN THE MONTHS after Sean died, as I emerged from numbness, I began to catch hold of Sean unexpectedly in ways that I could bear. Little boys raced each other to the school bus, making me laugh as well as yearn. The newborn next door became a chunky, red-haired toddler, delighting me with his good-natured stubbornness. Groups of adolescent males barged past me on the subway, and I felt invigorated by the sheer energy of the pack.

Six months ago a new comic strip called "Zits" appeared in our local paper. The title character is a tall, gangly teenage boy, a sometime musician with a loyal buddy, an occasional girlfriend and long-suffering parents. The artist has caught with humor and style the body language, monosyllabic verbal putdowns, facial grimaces, and the passions and agonies of an adolescent male. I now look for it every morning, often laughing out loud. There's a poignant undercurrent, but mostly it's fun to recapture my experience as mother to a teenage son.

My grandsons bring back Sean in happy bursts of recognition. The shock of a newborn penis, unexpectedly large on a tiny body. The strength of Will's legs, and then Hunter's—their refusal to collapse, as Sarah and Ashley's did, but Sean's didn't. Will's belly laugh in response to the two Labrador retrievers whom he delights in as big siblings. Sean was mesmerized by his sisters, christening them both "Sashley" as soon as he could talk. The pale polka-dot rash on Hunter's fair skin, reminiscent of Sean's red chin, chronically irritated by his nonstop drool. Will's preoccupation, at fourteen months, with any kind of ball.

Our suburban block has become a play street for a group of pre-teens, mostly boys, who play street hockey daily. I love their energy, their rough language, their alternating gruffness and sweetness, even their fury. I remember hauling Sean in from the street when he was about ten, appalled by the string of invectives that had just erupted from him. He was still writhing in outrage at his friend's injustice. "But, Mom," he sputtered, "you told me to use my mouth and not my hands."

I'VE DISCOVERED that I'm rich in kinesthetic memory, carried more in my body than in my mind. Photos of Sean are painful in their visual intensity, pulling me too rapidly from pleasure to loss. But when I capture him in other boys, I give in to the pleasure. I move again with the rhythm of being with him, a rhythm that cannot be stilled.

Some things remain too hard: his Ultimate Frisbee teammates, playing without him; a young musician, cradling the electric bass with surprising tenderness; a cousin's son, whom I haven't seen for years, whose carved cheekbones and warm grin under shoulder-length hair catch me off-guard. I startle, taste the intensity of my hunger for Sean, then retreat into a protected but less feeling place where I can watch, as if through the glass in a frame.

When my daughters became pregnant, within a few months of each other in 1997, I was thrilled. But I was also worried. I feared that the poignancy of a new boy in the family would flood me with longing and sorrow, and I hoped for granddaughters.

William Sean Ryan Gaddis was born to Ashley and Steve February 12, 1998, two and a half years after Sean's death. Hunter Lee Wieman, who was also named after Sean, was born six months later, on August 27, to Sarah and Rob. I marveled from the beginning at how reminiscent the babies were of my own, and yet how distinctly they were themselves. I gave up the nagging worry that they would be "replacement children," growing up too much in the shadow of the uncle they would never know. Alone with one of them, I sometimes wept because I could no longer hold my own son. But more often—as the babies engaged, frustrated and charmed me—I reveled in the ways that they reawakened the tactile and nonverbal music of my relationship with Sean.

This past December, the babies' first Christmas, the season of birth and rebirth, I began to play with poetry. It was as if the birth of the little boys awakened something new and unexpected in me. In my first poems I struggled to express both the wonder and the grief of the season: from "Christmas Morning": "Will in the high chair presiding… / he laughs, spreading cottage cheese and joy." And from "The Day after Christmas": "I wake up swollen / a damp, fertile grief / wanting to burst. // Carrying my dead child / I am bereft, but not barren…."

Just last month, in a leap of courage that took me by surprise, I registered for a class in poetry writing. In my first stab at a villanelle, I'm writing "Ultimate Frisbee Nationals, 1995: Sean's Last Game." Although I cannot bear to watch his teammates play without him, I find that as I begin to write I reexperience the thrill of watching Sean on the field: "You're reaching for the disc, I see you leap/and grasp it, score the point, look back at us and grin."

My grief is indeed fertile. In every corner of my mind, memories tumble unbidden across time, searching for a link, looking to unfold. I dip into one as I write, moving with it, and feeling its joy as I bring Sean back to life. As I translate my visceral memory into a formal, verbal one, I recapture my delight, discovering that I cannot succumb to sorrow while I am creating Sean anew on the page. It is the helplessness I feel when I stare at a photo that's unbearable, leaving me frightened that an essential part of me has died as well. But I write from a place in myself that is very much alive. Sitting at my keyboard, fingers in motion, I return to the wet grass of the playing field at Sean's Frisbee game and watch him emerge, not only in my mind, but in my words. I feel a suspension of grief, and a deep joy in that time that Bill and I shared with him. Sadness may come later, but my capacity to give birth to him in a new way remains.

Sean doesn't live in photographs. He lives within me. The comic strip, the boys on the street, and my grandsons quicken and nourish my relationship with him. And so do my memories, when I bring him alive in prose or poetry.

I know boys. I know boys in a way that I could not have known them without Sean. That knowledge enlivens the part of me that could imagine being a boy, and sometimes wanted to be. I realize with relief that as much as I treasure my photos of him, Sean lives in the melodies within me that I could not sing before I knew him. Sometimes I feel a tapping, a tune, a link and an unexpected happiness. I may find myself humming a song that he and

I sang together. Or I may even begin to hum a new song of my own, inspired by Sean, that I did not know before he died. Little by little, as I put words to my melodies, I'm learning to sing them out loud.

VIII

TALKING
WITH BILL

A s i step onto the porch, after six hours at my office listening to patients, Bill is carrying pork chops with rosemary from the grill to the table. It's twilight. I take my seat and watch the sailboats moored upriver at the boat club rock in the gentle current. As the glow of the summer evening fades, the deep blue of the water darkens. Bill opens a chilled bottle of wine.

"One of my young clients is getting married this weekend," I begin, trying to sound casual. "She and her mother went to a spa together yesterday. It reminded me of a day that Ashley and I spent in New York City about ten days before her wedding. After the final fitting for her wedding dress, we lingered over lunch, finalizing the seating at the reception. I remember laughing a lot. I feel sad that Sarah and I didn't have a day like that. The weeks before her wedding were so clouded by Sean's death."

Bill puts down his fork, reaching for the portable phone. "I'm going to call Ashley and Steve and tell them what fun we had at their house last weekend." He dials their number, and in a few moments he is speaking enthusiastically into their answering machine.

Struggling with feelings of being cut off, but uncertain what to say next, I concentrate on cutting my chop. I'm sure that Bill picked up the phone precisely because he did hear me. But instead of sharing my sorrow, he moved to his pleasure in our Fourth of July holiday with Sarah and Ashley and their families. I try to respect his need to do that. But it is hard, not only because tonight I want him to listen, but because this is a longtime dance between us. Bill tends to avoid the turbulence of his most difficult feelings. I stay silent, not wanting to bludgeon him with my psychological theories, which he hates. Finally, I start again, choosing my words carefully.

"When I mentioned Sean, you turned off your feelings right away and reached for the phone. I don't think you realize you did that."

Bill gazes out at the river. I sense that he feels stung, although his face is impassive. Finally, he turns back to me.

"No, I didn't realize it." He looks chagrined.

"I'm not asking for a lot. Just ten seconds of a response would be enough. Reach over and squeeze my hand, maybe."

He doesn't say any more. Disappointed by his silence, I sip my wine slowly and manage to bite my tongue. If I keep going, he'll feel attacked. "Do you want dessert?" I ask, reaching to clear his plate. "I'll put the kettle on for tea."

SEAN HAS BEEN dead almost four years. Will it ever be easier, I wonder, to share our saddest feelings with each other? A child's death shatters a family, leaving shards of loss everywhere. As time passes, I step into my grief at unexpected moments, and one of them was in the session with my young client. As I listened to her account of her day at the spa with her mother, I was reminded that Sarah and I didn't have a chance to share a lighthearted schoolgirl pleasure in the days before she was married.

I want to tell Bill about it, but I would settle for a brief acknowledgment. If he responded with too much feeling, I'd push down mine. Savoring a good dinner on our porch at the end of the day is one of the rituals of our life that calms me, reminding me of what we still have. Perhaps more important—I can't hold my own grief and his as well. I love him too much, and I know that the depth of his loss mirrors my own.

We each circle our own sorrow, unsure of its limits, wanting but not wanting to talk to each other about it.

Shared sorrow can be frightening. What if together we unleash a terrible, suffering beast that grows too large for us to contain? What if, like Max in *Where the Wild Things Are*, we shout "Be still!" but our demons do not obey?

I weep in my therapist's office, sometimes for a long time. Bill tells me that he grieves more with his own therapist than with me. After Sean died I was troubled because we rarely cried together, fearing that signaled a profound failure of intimacy. I think about it differently now. He and I both are afraid that talking together about this most exquisite of wounds risks harming each of us further.

Scar tissue has developed, but there is a layer of raw grief within each of us. In the months after Sean died, I sometimes thought of Bill, Sarah, Ashley and me as burn victims, all in need of intensive care. Hugging each other risked causing more agony: If I touch you where I still hurt, I thought—and where you hurt—we both hurt more, not less. I can bear my own pain—just barely—but I'm not certain that I can bear yours as well. We are all still careful, touching each other's sorrow gingerly, or not at all.

I can tap my pain more easily in the presence of someone outside our circle of four. My therapist is like the most skilled and compassionate of nurses: acutely sensitive to my pain, but not daunted by it. I wish that I could offer Bill more comfort. I can touch him in the rare moments when he cries with me, but sometimes I see such a bereft look in his eyes that I can't bear it, and I break the spell of feeling by changing the subject. He does the same. My capacity to stay with him when he grieves is a little better than his to stay with me—but not much.

The books on loss of a child tell us that many marriages do not survive. Ours has in fact become stronger —we each carry a profound knowledge of the other's courage in the face of disaster. For months after Sean died, we were gentle with each other, acutely conscious that any slights between us paled beside the engulfing hurt that we shared. Little by little our familiar bickering returned, an ironic reflection of some kind of healing. But our comradeship has deepened; we are fellow survivors of a flash fire that has left our family still picking its way among the embers.

SOMETIMES I WRITE what I cannot speak. And sometimes Bill reads what he cannot hear me speak. I begin by retreating to my study's cozy space, prompted by an urgency of emotion, and a fear of its boundlessness. Whether my tool is pen or keyboard, the movement of my fingers calms me, and I am able to dip into the unwieldy flow of feeling, transform it into words, capture it on the page. I may weep as I write. I don't yet know if I can reveal my fear, sadness or despair to another. But little by little, as I shape my writing further, I want to share it with Bill.

My own suffering beast breathes more softly for a while. I offer what I have written to him, and he always wants to read it. Sometimes not right away. But he will come back to it and be moved. I have separated my deepest pain from his, but I have also created a bridge between us, and he is grateful. He wants a way into his feelings, and he wants to know mine and to share them. Sometimes he cries or speaks and offers me a glimpse into his.

I SPENT AN AFTERNOON last weekend organizing photographs of our two grandsons. Browsing through old albums, I found newborn photos of Sarah, Ashley and Sean, and added them to our first album of grandchildren. Flipping back and forth and checking family resemblances was fun. But after three hours immersed in my task, I was exhausted. I recognized an aching fatigue that I lived with daily in the months after Sean died, when simple tasks seemed to consume all my energy.

I found Bill working in the garden. When I told him what I had been doing, he put down his trowel and looked up to scan my face quickly. "Did it make you sad?" he asked.

"Yes," I said, "but I didn't realize it until I finished."

He knows, I thought, that remembering is never simple anymore. I was glad that he was tuned in enough to ask the question, but this time I was the one who didn't want to talk about it. The afternoon was humid, with no breeze from the river to bring relief, and Bill's face was streaked with dirt. "You look hot," I said. "I'll get you some seltzer. Shall I check the movie schedule?"

Bill wiped his brow and smiled. "Good idea," he replied.

IX

LIVINGSTON
CLINIC

I T S NOT TOO BAD," says Kristen, the young physician's assistant at the clinic in Livingston, the small Montana town to which we drove from the trailhead. "There's a small puncture wound. Did you fall on a rock?"

"Yes," I answer. I can feel the tension in my voice.

"I'll clean it up as best I can," Kristen continues, in a matter-of-fact but friendly tone. She has short brown curls, a warm smile and gentle hands. "And I'll give you an antibiotic to protect against infection. Puncture wounds are difficult to clean. I'll take one stitch, since it's on your knee, so you won't have to worry about bending it. I'll numb it first. Okay?"

Lying prone on the examining table, I nod, too shaky to speak. "Are you all right?" Kristen asks.

I'm on the verge of sobbing, having trouble catching my breath. I gasp, and begin to cry. Kristen looks alarmed.

"It's not about my knee," I say. "Would you get my husband from the waiting room?" Barbara, the nurse with whom I chatted earlier about her adolescent daughter, is standing beside me, ready to assist Kristen.

"Sure," she replies. "What's his name?"

"Bill," I answer through my tears. She returns with him, and I grasp his hand, but I can't stop crying.

"It's not about my knee," I say again.

"I know," he replies softly. He looks stricken, as I give in to my sobs. After a few minutes I'm able to speak to the women who are still bent over my knee: "Our son, Sean, was killed in the mountains four years ago. Yesterday was the anniversary of his death."

"It's all right," answers Barbara. "I'll see if I can find a tissue."

"Try to think about something else," urges Bill. His eyes have clouded over, and I can see his mouth tighten as he speaks. He's worried that he'll break down, too.

"No," I respond quickly. "I need to cry."

Overtaken by my grief, I feel the relief of yielding to it. This week has been harder than I've wanted to acknowledge. We're in Montana with Ashley, Steve and Will, now eighteen months old. This morning we climbed a muddy, rock-strewn trail that Bill and Sean hiked eight years ago. I was enchanted by Will, who doggedly put one little foot in front of the other until the grown-ups tired of his pace, and insisted that he ride in his carrier. He quickly adapted to its comfort and bounce, amusing himself by playing with Steve's hat while munching raisins that Ashley dug from her pack.

We hiked up through a forest alongside a clear, cold mountain river, then into more barren, open landscape from which we could see distant mountain peaks. Memories of my earlier trip in the Tetons with Sean flowed like a soft, pleasurable current. As the five of us ate lunch next to a steep gravel slope, punctuated by boulders, we held tight to Will against his protests, because the grassy slope on which we sat was steep. He's eager to master new terrain, and he fought our constraints. My worry about him and the cap of snow on a far-off mountain triggered thoughts about Sean's plummet down the glacier, but I managed to keep those thoughts oddly distant and non-threatening.

On the way down the mountain we were caught in a thunderstorm. It rained hard, and tiny pellets of hail drummed our heads. Will cried at first, but clad in a hooded yellow slicker, he nestled like a small duck between his father's shoulders, and fell asleep. Although we were in a relatively protected area in the forest, I was nervous. We moved as rapidly as possible on the increasingly mud-slicked trail. The muscles in my legs quivered, prompting me to say, "We have to slow down a little. I'm afraid I'll trip."

As the storm abated, the path became less steep and I relaxed a little. Suddenly, I fell—hard. I found myself sprawled on the ground on my knees, my hands on the trail, too, protecting my face. Slowly, I made my way to a sitting position in the mud and surveyed my knees for signs of injury. At first I saw dirt but no blood. Bill looked carefully at my legs, and we both saw blood oozing from a small laceration in my right knee, then some yellow gunk. I turned away quickly, feeling faint. "You'll need a stitch," Bill said calmly. He looked at Steve. "Do you have the first-aid kit?" Steve dug it out of the side pocket of Will's carrier.

Bill carefully cleaned my wound with a diaper wipe, working slowly to minimize the sting. He covered the laceration with a clean piece of gauze, taped it and wrapped an ace bandage around my knee to help me keep it straight. We had another forty-five minutes of hiking before us.

"Take your time," he said gently. "We don't have to hurry."

I tried to remember the rhythm of Lamaze breathing, steadied myself mentally, took a drink of water and got back on my feet. No real pain. I started down the slope, moving somewhat stiffly and slowly, but I felt relieved and was beginning to see this as an adventure, even a story to tell. Will slept soundly. We waded carefully across the river, not bothering to take off our boots, already soaked through in the storm. My ace bandage was bloody by the time we reached the car.

We headed straight for Livingston and were directed to the local medical clinic, where Kristen and Barbara are working intently on my knee. If they are unnerved by what I said, they don't reveal it. When their work is finished, Kristen leaves, saying, "I'll check back," and Barbara stays with us. My sobs have abated, but I'm shaking uncontrollably. Bill takes off my wet boots and socks, and Barbara covers me with a cotton blanket.

"Where were you hiking?" she asks.

I appreciate her kindness, and her professionalism, but I long for her to ask about Sean. *What happened? How was he killed? How old was he? Tell me about him. Tell me about Sean.*

I yearn to talk about Sean. About six months after he died, I went cross-country skiing in Vermont with a group of women. A college classmate, whom I hadn't seen for over thirty years, was there. "Tell me about Sean," she said. I was so grateful.

"He was tall," I answered, "with broad shoulders and long legs, and his pants always rested on his hip bones. He smiled easily and loved to laugh. He was smart, and even when he was little he could talk circles around me. In high school he learned to play the bass, and in college he became a scholar. He was passionate about Ultimate Frisbee, biking miles up and down the hills in Santa Cruz to strengthen his muscles for rock climbing. He adored his older sisters and talked often in the months before he died about coming east for Sarah and Rob's wedding in the fall.

"He was gentle and warm and he called me 'Ma.' Neither of the girls ever called me 'Ma.'"

Before Sean died I talked about him often. People would ask, "Where's Sean? What's he doing this summer?" Obviously, they don't ask those questions anymore. But I think Barbara and Kristen would have asked what happened to him if some uneasiness hadn't stopped them. Do they think I might not stop crying? Surely, they've been around sobbing patients before. I read once that you can literally die of hiccups if they can't be stopped, but I don't think that's true of sobbing. Barbara does say to us, "I can't imagine. I have three children, and I can't imagine losing one of them."

"We have two others," I reply, "and two thriving little grandsons." I feel compelled to tell her that we're okay. What I'm aching to say is this: *Our daughter Ashley is writing a memoir of Sean. I'm so moved by her memories of her younger brother, and her reflections on whether she, our middle child, is still a big sister, now that he's gone.* And I wanted to say this: *I still want so badly for Sean to come home. I hate the anniversary of his death, and when it's over and I think I've survived, I'm unexpectedly blindsided by sadness. Sometimes I'm the one who's afraid that if I start to cry I won't stop.*

It's easy for me to blame others for not inquiring. *Why don't you ask me how I am? Why don't you mention Sean anymore? Don't you think of him, too? If I speak of our grief, why are you silent?* I could, after all, just keep talking. But maybe that would be rude or pushy, and I'd make the other person uncomfortable. I'd be breaking the rules of polite conversation.

When I write I can break the rules. I can insist on my words, on saying what I like, on not protecting others from my pain or my wish to inflict it on them. Sometimes I just want to hurl it around.

You take some of it. I'm sick of hurting. I'm sick of tears, especially the ones that are stuck in my throat. I'm sick of waking up hourly at night on the verge of a nightmare. I'm sick of the daily struggle of living without him. I'm sick of smiling at other young men's weddings and of being courteous when careless friends ask, "Is everyone coming home?" I wonder how reckless and cruel my words could be: *"Actually, Sean won't be able to make it. Ever."*

My fury collapses into a cry. *Where are you, Sean? I need you to come home.*

Sometimes on a summer night, when the windows are open, I hear the furious yelping bark of a small animal, then the rise and fall of a desperate high-pitched wail. I pour my words onto the page because I'm afraid of the sounds of my own anguish.

IN MONTANA my anguish blows through me like a quick, violent storm. Bill's tenderness and touch and the care of the women help to quiet me. When I leave the clinic, I feel exhausted and melancholy, but calmer. An urgency grows in me to return home to the safety of my study, to write down everything that happened today.

A few days later, after a difficult goodbye to Ashley, Steve and Will, I soothe myself on the flight back to New York by beginning an essay in my mind. When I've put it on paper, and mastered the story, I'll be able to reclaim the pleasures of the hike—our conversation with Ashley and Steve, our amusement at Will, the splendor of the mountain scenery, even pride in weathering a nasty fall.

ON THE PLANE I'll also think about Ashley, whose book draft is unfinished. She's struggling to carve out time to write, now that she has Will to care for. I'd hate for her to let it go, especially since this summer I've been thinking more and more about writing a book myself. I've already written half a dozen essays, and have made some forays into publishing several of them. Why not a book? This thought still seems bold, but I know there's a need for a book that maps the terrain of a surviving parent in a real way, over a period of years. That tells one mother's story. That doesn't speak of closure. That tells how hard the journey is, and how long—but how mixed up it is, as well—with experiences that can bring surprising happiness.

I don't want to overshadow Ashley, who was a writer before I became one. She wrote a class play in high school, an opinion column for her college newspaper, and was working as a reporter in Fort Collins when Sean died. The following spring she finished her master's degree in journalism at the University of Colorado. Soon after his death, she talked about writing a memoir of Sean. I was proud of her, but unexpectedly envious—maybe the first sign of my own wish to write. Once I began my essays, I worried about what it would mean to her if I published them.

Little by little I realized that I couldn't—or wouldn't—silence myself. When I first began writing, I didn't always speak freely to Ashley about it. But about a year ago I found a time to talk with her. We were hiking a woodland trail near our home in Nyack. "How do you feel about my writing?" I asked her. She paused, probably caught off guard.

"I've thought about it," she answered carefully. "Since I was a kid, I wanted something in the family that only I did. I thought writing would be it. But now Dad's working on his book about the Black Sea, and you're thinking about publishing some of your essays, or even a book. At first I felt bad, but I'm realizing that maybe writing is a tradition in the family—Dad has always written papers—and maybe that's one reason I'm a writer. I've been thinking that what's important is that what I write is in my voice, and no one else's. And I'm happy for you, and relieved that you've found something that helps you."

IF ASHLEY'S CONFIDENCE that there's room for both of us is uncertain, she never acknowledges it. Occasionally, I still worry that my own ambition as a writer is causing my daughter pain. Maybe a better mom would leave that territory to her. But I have discovered something of my own that I refuse to give up. It is part of my fight for my own life.

IX

A ROOM IN
MY MIND

I DREAM THAT HUNTER has been to the allergist, subjected to an invasion of pinpricks and needles, and that he's still allergic to many foods. He will need allergy shots. What Sarah hopes will nourish him could turn out to be toxic instead. I'm frightened for him, wondering in my dream if his allergies will continue indefinitely, in spite of the doctor's initial optimism that he would become less allergic over time.

I wake up perplexed. In fact, Sarah has just learned that Hunter has outgrown most of his allergies. At fifteen months he's now digging into everything, relishing his meals and gaining weight.

I know that dreams are often about the dreamer. Are there ways, I wonder, in which I feel allergic, subjected to invasion? The holidays are approaching, and I've begun to feel the beginning of depression. I look forward to the warmth of people gathering together, but without Sean

I also feel a sense of dread and fatigue, of something being taken from each of us and all of us every holiday season.

Before he died, thoughts of Sean nurtured me. This time of year I looked forward with excitement to his arrival home for Christmas. Now I feel disrupted, poked and prodded by thoughts and memories that interrupt my anticipation of a holiday that I've loved since I was a small child. I taste Sean's presence daily, but I have trouble savoring it. If I'm able to enjoy it today, I'm still uneasy, wondering if tomorrow I will feel sick with sadness.

FROM THE TIME my children were infants, they got under my skin in ways both satisfying and disturbing. I would immerse myself in caring for them, then long for release. The pleasure of nursing a newborn would evolve into a restless wish to reclaim my body for myself. The enjoyment of snuggling with a baby who had awakened in the night would turn into a longing for her to fall asleep so I could return her to her crib. The excitement of being greeted in the morning by a toddler calling "Mommy," when language was new, would soon be tempered by weariness at the daily litany of cries for me.

If I decided to take time out and hire a babysitter, I'd be distracted all day by an image of tearful faces when I said goodbye. On my return the children would be content, and I would wish that my distress were as short-lived as theirs. I was enchanted by how rapidly their language developed, and fascinated by the complexity of my daughters' dollhouse play, or by Sean's block cities for his Matchbox cars. But when they whined or fought, refused to eat, or had temper tantrums at bedtime, I felt drained. I had difficulty coming to terms with my anger at them, and my wish to escape their demands and provocations. As they grew up, this struggle within myself took different forms, sometimes exploding into clashes with them.

When Sean was about twelve, and almost my height, I asked him to help me with a kitchen chore. He paused on the way upstairs to his room, turned to me, and said rudely, "Why do I have to do everything around here?"

I was infuriated by his tone, as well as by the absurdity of his statement. His face was only inches from mine, and I shocked us both by slapping him across the cheek. He stood for a moment stunned, then turned and raced upstairs to his room, slamming the door behind him. I must have apologized later, although I don't remember doing so. I do remember that he kept a distance from me for a few days, and I was glad.

After Sean died, I thought about that slap. I realized that although I wasn't proud of it, I didn't regret it either.

He had clearly been insolent. I resented his invasion, and my reaction was impulsive but clear: "Get out of my face."

GRIEF HAS A RELENTLESS and stubborn quality that invades me in a very different way. My awareness of Sean's absence, now that he is dead, is more pervasive than my awareness of his presence was when he was alive. I think or dream about him every day, unable to escape the anguish of his no longer being in the world. He is as intertwined with me as he was when I carried him in my womb. Now I carry him in my mind, and once again he has no separate existence. His death, ironically, has collapsed the space between us.

Ashley told us last month that she is expecting her second baby in May, and Sarah just revealed that she, too, is pregnant. Her baby's birthday will be in June, just a few days from Sean's. I'm so pleased that my daughters' families are growing, but I wonder how much my anticipation of Sean's birthday will temper my excitement about the new babies. Bill and I are planning to rent a house on Cape Cod next August to share with our daughters and their families. The fifth anniversary of Sean's death falls within that time and I'm glad that we'll be together, but I wonder how sad and depleted I'll be. Sometimes I resent the toll that grief takes on my relationships with the living.

I will always carry Sean, but I don't want to be invaded by him. I can set a boundary between myself and my living daughters: "No, we can't come this weekend." "I'm going upstairs to take a nap." Or to Bill, "Thank God that visit is over." I can give in to the urgency of my wish to be separate, secure in the knowledge that Sarah and Ashley will be waiting for me when I want to be together again. But can I free myself, just for a little while, from the claims of my dead son?

IF I LET GO of Sean, if I push him away, I'm no longer sure that he'll be there waiting for me. I feel despairing, but I also feel angry. I go to my study and I put my fingers to the keyboard. I immerse myself in words, and I confess the other side of my passion for him—a ruthless wish that sometimes he would keep his distance. I write quickly through my tears, not sure that I will ever print these words: "Sean's shadow lies across the family. We cannot keep him alive.... Keeping him alive is a metaphor. He is not alive. We cannot hear his voice, see him, touch him, smell him.... We cannot even worry about him, we can no longer have hopes for him.... But he will not go away either.... I cannot live with him now that I must live without him."

SLOWLY, A NEW AWARENESS is emerging. I'm bringing Sean to life in my journals and rekindling my relationship with him as well. Our relationship continues, as I try to make it work somehow, even though he's no longer physically in my world. I am creating him and us anew, in a place that is both mine and separate from me.

Me and not-me. Like a child's blanket, my journal is my confidant, full of sadness and rage and despair, of hope and discouragement, of tears and comfort. When a toddler cries into her blanket, or hugs it with an almost sensual pleasure, or bites into it in fury, she is clutching a kind of pre-verbal diary that is a bridge to her mother, but also to her own emotions. She can put it aside when she doesn't need it, and reclaim it when she does.

When I write, I create something that can't be destroyed, except by me. It is a link to Sean, and a link to my love and yearning, my anger and despair. My first words, which I write uncensored if I dare, remain part of my journal. My essays become something else. As I polish and rework my most primitive thoughts, I create a story, which links me to others and assures Sean's place in the world beyond mine. Perhaps if I'm sure that he remains safe outside my mind, I can give up my preoccupation with him. I'm not yet sure about that.

What I do know is that as I emerge as a writer I'm becoming stronger in my autonomy, in my willingness to be my own person. A little girl's blanket is a first act of creation: a symbol. However inspired by a relationship, it is her own. And so it is with what I have written.

Writing is pulling me away from a life defined by my involvement with others—my husband, my children, my clients. As enriching as that life has been, I've felt held hostage to it as well, perpetually conscious of my responsibility to others. I'm discovering that I love the freedom of being alone with my ideas and my keyboard, however frustrating or painful that time may be.

Something of myself, still nascent, was nourished in the wake of Sean's death. My writing is not just a link to myself, or to Sean, or a way of sharing him with the world. Most of all, it is about me. My growing determination to turn my essays into a book is about my wish to expose myself—my feelings, my ideas and my way of weaving words. It is also a reflection of my understanding that I cannot rely on others to define my life. I won't give up my fierce attachment to those I love, but I need not only a room in my house, but also a room of my own in my mind: a place to go when I feel overwhelmed by loss, but also where I can play and grow.

I'M FIGHTING HARDER than ever for the right to my own life, separate from my children. Early in my life as a mother, I could feel how essential that was. It was just as important for them to become separate from me. When Sean chose college in California, a friend asked: "How can you let him go so far away?"

"How can I not let him?" I replied.

"Do you worry about him?" another asked, when I told her that he was working as a ranger on Mount Rainier.

"Yes," I answered. But I never thought that I had the right to ask him not to climb.

Sean chose to climb. Occasionally, I wonder if his choosing something dangerous had to do in part with asserting his independence from me. I've always been terrified of physical risks, and I secretly loved his willingness to take them. I've wondered if my deep pride in his strength and courage kept me from recognizing how dangerous his climbing really was. Maybe I could have been more clear with him about that danger.

I always knew that my pride in him was an attempt to borrow for myself Sean's energy, strength and bravery. I realize now that, ironically, it was also a way of denying our separateness. I don't have Sean to take risks for me anymore, and I find myself stretching my own autonomy. I'm discovering that my own willingness to take risks lies not in the physical realm but in the world of words.

XI
FIVE YEARS
LATER

B ILL AND I are standing on a grassy knoll in the cemetery on Cape Cod with Sarah and Ashley, Rob and Steve. A tiny urn of Sean's ashes is buried here with those of his grandparents. A loose bouquet of hydrangeas from my sister Susan's garden—huge puffballs of blue, purple and creamy white petals—lies between two headstones, one inscribed with the names of Bill's parents, the other inscribed "Sean Hunter Ryan." Sarah turns to me. "Would you like me to read the poem?" she asks.

"Yes," I say. "If you can."

She begins, speaking softly but clearly, only a slight tremor to her voice:

"These are the rocks he loved when he was alive...."

I begin to cry, and my weeping intensifies as she continues:

"And how alive he was, like the sun this afternoon
Making mica gleam on the old face of granite...

"So that I still believe in him as in the sun,
And expect him to reappear as winter passes...."

I WOKE UP this morning dreading the day, wishing that it
were over. This fifth anniversary of Sean's death is the first
August 12 that the rest of us have all been together since
our trip to Mount Rainier. I'm so grateful to Sarah for
reading the poem that I chose. She is thirty-three, her red
hair now cropped in a young mom cut, which highlights
her small features and adds sophistication to her youthful
face. Her belly is still slightly rounded and her breasts are
full. Rob stands next to her, holding Eliza, swaying gently
back and forth, appearing to soothe himself as well as the
baby. Laurel is sleeping in the car, parked nearby, windows
open so Ashley and Steve can hear her if she cries. We have
left Will and Hunter, now active two-year-olds, with
Susan, who lives in a neighboring town.

I hold my body still, trying to contain my sobs,
although tears are running down my face. Bill stands
beside me, but I find it difficult to look at him. His eyes
glisten and his mouth is working in a way that I know too
well by now. The sky is gray and the air is damp. Grave-
stones are scattered over the rolling green hillsides of the
cemetery, shaded by large old trees.

I'VE KNOWN FOR MONTHS that I wanted to mark the milestone of five years in some way, but a familiar numbing exhaustion would drain me whenever I tried to focus on what to do. I could only think as far as including this poem. I thought immediately of Sean when I first came upon it, and I wanted to show it to Bill and to our daughters. Its poignancy made that hard, and I veered away from the intimacy of exposing my own grief, and of eliciting theirs.

A few days ago Sarah gave me an opening. "Do you know what you want to do on August 12?" she asked, adjusting Eliza at her breast. She and I were sitting in the kitchen of the cottage in Wellfleet which Bill and I had rented for the family for two weeks. Beyond the adjoining deck the pungent grasses of the marsh shimmered in the unexpected sunshine of this cool, wet summer.

"We're here on the Cape," I answered. "I'd like to visit the gravesite, and have some kind of remembrance there." I paused. "I brought a poem I love, but I won't be able to read it without coming undone."

Sarah looked up at me. "Maybe someone else could read it. I'd like to see it." Then she added gently, "Maybe it's okay if you come undone."

"Maybe so," I said, but I sounded unconvinced, even to myself.

The next day, Bill and I took a walk at the nearby Audubon center with her and Rob and their children. The day was breezy and slightly overcast, the pale green marsh grass waving softly as it ran to the darker sea. Bill and Rob walked ahead to the beach with Hunter, and Sarah, who carried Eliza tucked into her Snugli, turned to me. "Do you feel listened to in the family if you want to talk about Sean?" she asked. I paused, touched by her question, but not sure how to answer it.

"Yes," I said, slowly. "Mostly I do… and I do by you and Ashley, although sometimes not by Dad. If I don't talk about my grief it is because…" I paused again, not sure what to say or how to say it. "Sometimes it's about not wanting to upset you and Ashley, or burden you with how I feel."

Sarah didn't respond, and I sensed that she was waiting for me. I struggled to figure it out, and to put into words what I don't understand altogether myself. Yes, I want to protect my daughters, to give them freedom from worry about a grieving mother, or believing that their dead brother pre-occupies her. But there is more.

"Going there myself is hard—going to how I feel. Talking about Sean, remembering Sean, even thinking about how much I miss him is too intense… it doesn't comfort me—I want him back too much."

I was crying, talking much less coherently than I write. Sarah dug a packet of tissues out of her pocket for me. "With Grandmommy and Grandfather it's different. I've accepted that they're gone, and I feel happy when I remember them. But with Sean, remembering just breaks my heart. I can sometimes tell stories about him, especially about when he was a little boy. But I'm kind of removed from him when I do. I don't know how to *feel* him without wanting him back more than I can bear." I coughed, and blew my nose fiercely. I could hear anger as well as anguish in my voice. "I don't think that will ever change."

Sarah's eyes were filling, but she didn't flinch. We were still walking, headed back to the car by then. Bill and Rob kept a distance behind us with Hunter, although we could still hear the sound of his happy chatter.

In our family there is always a reluctance to move in without an invitation. But in her quiet way Sarah had persisted. We had each survived my talking and weeping —my coming undone. From inside, my feelings seemed so large and raw that I feared they would overwhelm both of us. When Hunter is weeping uncontrollably, and Sarah says to him, "Use your words," she is teaching him that big feelings can become manageable when spoken out loud. In the horror of losing Sean, I lost that assurance.

Sarah and I have a history of struggling with our feelings —and sometimes with each other—in writing. So it seemed natural early on to speak to her about my grief by sharing with her what I had written. Responding to *Journey to Mount Rainier*, she wrote back to me three years ago: "Your writing gave me… reassurance that your experiences, while awful were not unspeakable…. I felt the piece gave me a window into your grieving, something I had both wanted and was scared of, and after reading your… descriptions of your experience I didn't feel scared, just more deeply connected."

On our walk that day she invited me into a closeness unmediated by the written page, and I felt relieved and appreciative.

I MORE OFTEN take a chance on talking about my sadness than my rage. I've always been afraid of my anger, which tends to lie dormant, turning into depression or an attack on someone I love, which surprises and hurts us both. My anger about Sean's death lives mostly in the background of my mind, less troubling and intrusive than my yearning. But, occasionally, it erupts inside me in short, furious bursts, which I rarely speak about. I try to capture it on paper instead.

Sean's diploma from UCSC hangs now in the third-floor guestroom that used to be his bedroom. Bill and I had it framed shortly after he died, and carefully hung it there. After we repainted the room last year, I put something else in its place. "Where's Sean's diploma?" Ashley asked, on one of her visits home.

"I felt angry every time I looked at it," I said, with an edge to my voice. Ashley looked taken aback.

"I kind of like it there," she responded. "But if you really don't, that's okay," she added quickly.

Always solicitous of my feelings, she's sometimes too quick to sacrifice her own. I thought about that and about the reality that she spends more time in that room than I do. I returned the diploma to its place. But one day my anger ballooned into an urge to take it off the wall and smash it into little bits on the rocks by the river. The pieces could float out to sea with Sean's ashes, I thought, and it would no longer taunt me with its empty promise.

I am taunted as well by a flag in the adjoining playroom, folded and encased in glass, which bears the inscription: "This flag flown at Mount Rainier National Park is presented to the family of Park Ranger Sean H. Ryan in his honored memory." I was startled when we received it, since I had not brought into focus Sean's status as a government employee who died in the line of duty. There seemed, in fact, to be a kind of black humor in the flag, since Sean was such a questioner of the establishment that if he had grown up in the sixties he might have burned one. I tucked the flag away in a closet, but Bill retrieved it and put it out on the bookshelf.

When I saw it there, I suddenly realized how much I'd like to chop up that flag and send it back in tatters to the rangers who sent Sean and Phil on their mission that night. I think of Sean's grit and determination in making his way up the glacier, steeling himself against fatigue and cold, no sounds but the whistle of wind, grunts of breath, the crunch of crampons. I am awed by his courage. But I am embittered by the hero story. Sean was killed by friendly fire, by the stupidity and poor judgment of his superiors. He was a brave young man, but he was too young and too inexperienced, and idealizing him as a hero lets those who should have known that off the hook. I'm furious because no one who was on the mountain that night has ever acknowledged to us any responsibility or regret for their part in the tragedy.

In a trunk in Sean's old room are the gloves that he was wearing when he died. Two right gloves—a huge, gray fleece mitten, and a navy blue shell, the pair designed to protect a climber's hand from the damage of frostbite. Sean's right hand was visible in his casket; his left hand, bare when he fell, was hidden from us. What can I do with those mitts? I can't imagine dropping them in the garbage. I wish we had put them in his coffin and cremated them, too.

The room that is now my study, my writing room, was Sean's room when he was a little boy. The woodwork is still trimmed, somewhat haphazardly, in blue paint. Bill was foolhardy enough to tell Sean that he and his best friend, Sean Iannucci, could help him paint the room. The boys were only six or seven, and they gabbed like two little girls, distracted, flipping paint everywhere.

We always called them "the two Seans." They met in nursery school, and Sean Iannucci's mother rescued our Sean from a babysitter he hated, offering to care for him herself on the days that I worked. The boys were each beautiful, one a sturdy fair-skinned blond with blue eyes, the other more slender, olive complected, with dark hair and deep brown eyes. Sean Iannucci is now married and the father of a baby daughter who looks so much like him that I laughed out loud when I opened the birth announcement. But then I wanted to rip it up. I am so sad and angry that our Sean was cheated of the opportunity to be a father.

Rolled up in the closet of my study is a huge banner, designed by a friend for Sean's memorial service in Nyack. The background is mountains against a brilliant blue sky, and emblazoned across it in gold letters are the words, "We love you, Sean." Whenever I dig into that closet for clothes or books, I come upon it. I wonder if we'll ever decide what to do with it, or if Sarah and Ashley will have to figure that out when we die. Maybe the banner will keep being passed down in the family because no one can bear to destroy it. When I think about that, I don't feel angry, just sad and defeated.

Sadness and defeat. They always overtake my anger, and they are stronger. No matter what we keep or don't keep, Sean is gone. Our grandchildren will not know him. They will each grow up with their own idea of Sean, constructed from family stories, photographs and other memorabilia, newspaper clippings, perhaps my essays. But however important he may be to any one of them, he will also be a lost and unknowable uncle, a phantom whose shadow they cannot escape, but who remains a mystery.

I DREAMED LAST WEEK that Sean was coming for dinner— only for dinner—then he would be gone again. In my dream I felt both excited anticipation and a terrible dread. I woke up, but I remained in a groggy, middle-of-the-night, post-dream state, pondering whether I could bear to have him come home, if I knew that he would leave again forever. When I awoke again in the morning, I lay in bed and I wondered what mother would hesitate to see her son just one more time—to hug him and feel the lean strength of his body, to touch his cheeks, to look into his eyes and memorize precisely their shade of blue, to hear again the timbre of his voice and the range of his laughter?

I am that mother! I couldn't stand to go through losing him again. Of course, I want him back—I want him back with every fiber of my being. But I want him back to stay. I want to be able to reach him by phone. I want him home for Christmas. Five years have passed—Sean would be twenty-eight now. I want to know what he would be doing, where he would be living. I want to see how his body would have matured, what the contours of his face would be. I want to know whether he would be engaged—or even married—and who that other woman in his life would be.

Sean's high school friend, Clarence, came over for lunch with Bill and me one day when he was home last summer. We ate sandwiches on our porch and we caught up with Clarence's life, and we talked about Sean. "He was so proud of his sisters," Clarence said. "He really loved his sisters. I remember in high school when Ashley's friends ganged up against her, and Sean was so upset. He was so angry at those girls." He paused. "I think about Sean every day," he said.

"How do you think about him?" I asked, my curiosity overcoming my reticence.

Clarence thought a minute. "I talk to him," he replied. "He was my buddy. He's still my buddy."

My eyes filled up, and I knew that I would cry if I tried to speak. How I envy Clarence his faith. I would like to feel Sean's presence in the way that he does. My son-in-law Steve tells me that he talks to Sean sometimes, and Ashley says that she likes to believe that Sean has a hand in the good things that happen to her. My own childhood faith in an afterlife faded long ago, years before Sean died. I don't talk to him. I don't believe that he can hear me.

Everyone who loves Sean carries him privately. I want to know where and how. If I had the courage, I would ask everyone he knew: *Where does Sean live in you? When do you think of him? How often? What do you miss?* When someone tells me a snippet of their thoughts or feelings about Sean, it's always a tease. At a family wedding this fall, my niece, Kim, hesitantly told Bill and me that she and her husband and brothers had been up late the night before reminiscing about Sean. As grateful as I was to her for telling us, I was hungry for more. How did he come up, I wondered, and what did they say? What stories did they tell? I'm sure that some of them were funny, and they all laughed, but did they also cry? I have a fierce wish to know how Sean is alive in other people's minds. Because this is where he lives now—in my mind, in Bill's mind, in his sisters' minds, in the minds of everyone who knew him.

Even though my glimpses inside others' minds are too few, memories of Sean remain vivid and bright in the windows of my own. I don't always find solace in them, but I do find relief from my fear of losing the intense color and heat of his aliveness. I have surges of grief that are searing, when he washes over me.

At a party Thanksgiving weekend, I sat near a table of young adults—two sisters and two brothers—and their husbands and wives. They seemed so at home with each other, and with each others' spouses. I was riveted by the two young men, enjoying the laughter between them and their sisters. Then I could feel my pleasure becoming an ache, and without thinking I looked away, as the ache turned to a painful craving for Sean.

But I also want that craving, because with it comes a memory of Sean laughing. Our family is sitting around the dining room table, and I can see Sean's grin widening, I can see him throw back his blond head, I can see him lean back in his chair and catch himself before he goes over, I can see his face redden and his eyes fill with tears because he can't stop laughing. It is harder to hear his laughter, but I can see his face, and I can see Sarah and Ashley's faces, and they are laughing, too.

XII
TALKING
WITH BILL
(Reprise)

THE FRONT DOOR slams behind Bill. He walks into the kitchen and riffles through the mail distractedly, barely saying hello. Earlier in the day, he had called to tell me that his dermatologist had found another squamous cell cancer that must be removed. The surgery can be extensive—the doctor doesn't know until he begins how far the malignant cells have traveled. Although we anticipate a good result, the procedure is an alarming reminder of Bill's susceptibility to skin cancers and our fears of a melanoma. This spot is near his hairline, an inch or so from his right eye. He looks up and says in a dejected tone, "Dr. Albom is going to cut up my face again."

He hates the scar from the last surgery, and fears that his face will be chipped away over time. I try to reassure him: "I can barely see the scar on your forehead anymore. It has faded almost entirely."

"I see it every morning in the mirror," he answers grimly. I look at Bill, and I think how handsome he still is—square-jawed, with even features that are animated by dimples when he smiles. He has a nicely proportioned straight nose, which I envy, since mine turns up at the end. Our daughters inherited my nose, and I find it charming on them, but silly on me. Sean's nose was more straight and serious, like Bill's. I never thought that they looked that much alike, but now I'm startled when I see certain photos, side by side, and realize how similar are the shapes of their faces, the tilts of their heads. Father and son each have grins that invite you in, and warm you with their openness and generosity. Although Sean wasn't arrogant, he was aware of his good looks, with a certain jauntiness to his vanity. Bill keeps his more under wraps. I know, however, how much he dreads this next medical assault. The aging process is insult enough.

He opens the refrigerator and rummages about. "Should I have a martini?" he asks, ice tray in hand. He usually opens a beer when he comes home in the evening. Martinis are an indulgence, for moments of celebration or stress only. He's looking for my permission.

"Why not?" I reply. Bill finds olives and vermouth, then goes to the liquor cupboard for gin. I hear the sound of ice cracking. He makes himself a drink, but doesn't settle down on a kitchen stool, as he often does. He's restless, wandering around the room.

"The Middle East battling was worse than ever today," he says suddenly. "Two Israeli soldiers were lynched. Israel destroyed Arafat's headquarters in retaliation. And an American ship was bombed by a suicide boat, killing at least half a dozen sailors. All those young men..." His voice trails off. He's watching me pull leftovers out of the refrigerator, along with a package of club steaks. "Shall I cook dinner?"

I realize that he wants to. I was looking forward myself to unwinding by chopping and sautéing, but I say, "Sure." He comes around to the stovetop and starts loudly foraging for pots and pans below. I get out of his way and begin to set the table in the dining room. We have trouble cooking as a team. In a few minutes, the smell of onions frying in butter accompanies the sizzle of meat. Butter makes Bill feel better. If he leaves the cooking to me, I'll use olive oil.

Twenty minutes later I light the candles and we sit down to steak, leftover pasta and frozen peas. Not bad for Thursday night, when food supplies are always low. Once it is too cool to eat on the porch, we eat dinner in the dining room. Bill and I both look forward to the ritual of a candlelit dinner at a nicely set table.

"I'm tired," Bill says, as he sits down. "Lee and I had a good run this morning, but it was early." He picked up his fork, then paused, and I saw something shift in his face. "You know... I run in Sean's windbreaker." I do know that. Bill appropriated for himself Sean's bright green, almost chartreuse jacket, when it arrived home from the West Coast. He wears Sean's watch every day, reluctantly replacing the wristband about a year ago, for fear the old one would break. He wears Sean's scrimshaw belt buckle, too, which he himself bought for Sean at a Nyack street fair—his last Christmas gift to Sean. I was with Bill when he bought it, and I remember his excitement about it. And I remember Sean's pleasure when he opened it, "Wow, Dad, this is really great... this is cool!"

"I think of Sean when I run," Bill continues thoughtfully. "When I pass under the streetlights before sunrise, my shadow lengthens, I become longer and leaner, and I see Sean. My gait is just like his. Then the shadow shifts and he is running away, running from me. It's symbolic, you think weird stuff." He shakes his head. "It's weird," he repeats.

I feel my eyes fill up. Bill rarely offers me such an opening into his most personal thoughts. I'm also intrigued by what he said. I can't find Sean in my own face or body, even though I know that Sean also looked like me, and that his height came more from my family than from Bill's. I do sometimes see him in Sarah or Ashley. Only once—at the hairdresser's, looking at myself in the mirror without my glasses—have I caught a glimpse of the bone structure of his face in mine.

As I listen to Bill, I'm in and out of my own worry about his skin cancer. Recently, I've been wrestling with my own fears of dying as well, brought to the forefront by a neighbor's critical illness, and I talked this week with my therapist about them. "For a while after Sean died, I was less afraid," I said. "I felt somehow that if he could do it, I could, too." I paused. That struck me as an odd thought. But Stefanie, who lost her husband two years ago, seemed to know what I meant.

"I felt the same way," she said. "I still do."

I shook my head. "I've lost that feeling," I said ruefully. "I wonder now if it was about not believing yet that Sean was gone, or that he could be that separate from me. Maybe it was about wanting to believe we would be together again, that I could find him on the other side. I *don't* believe that. And I'm just as scared of my own death now as ever."

I come out of my reverie, and begin to tell Bill what Stefanie and I were talking about. "Oh," he replies quickly, "I'm still less afraid. Knowing that Sean was willing to risk death, I feel more that I could, too."

"But Sean didn't believe that he was risking death when he started up the mountain," I counter quickly. "He was too full of youthful confidence and a sense of his own immortality."

"He knew he would die once he began to fall," Bill answers firmly.

I wince at the certainty in his tone. I've told myself that as long as Sean was fighting to re-engage his ice ax he had not given up hope. And I hold on to the belief that he and Phil were knocked unconscious within moments—or at the very least that their terror was tempered by the kind of shock and disconnection from reality that protected us when we first heard that he had died.

Bill stops eating altogether. "Not having the third guy on the rescue team... there should always be three... Mike Gauthier told me that. Two is not enough to make decisions... Phil had government issue equipment, not his own... It was error upon error." He looks away, then back at me. "Sean and I had talked about rescues. He knew they were the greatest risk. I had said to him, 'This is the biggest danger, because you are not calling the shots. The guy who is injured calls the shots.'"

He's looking into space, not at me, and I see him blink. I don't say anything, not wanting to interrupt his thoughts or his inclination to share them. His mind, like mine, is a storehouse of private memories and imaginings and I'm moved by a glimpse into it.

Bill shakes his head slowly. "You change, you think deeper, you think about things you didn't think about much before. It makes you richer." He pauses. "Not that you wouldn't trade it all in a minute to have him back."

I can't speak. I, too, have thought that I am richer—richer in knowledge of what the human heart can bear, and of what it can overcome, and of how much joy can enter even a heart still cracked. My grandchildren have taught me about the joy. And I am richer in a sense of connection to those parents—Israeli, Arab, American—whose sons are coming home in wooden boxes.

"It all came back," Bill is saying, "when I saw the paper today—the shock, and the unreality of being told... and all the steps in front of those families."

I THINK THAT Bill's healing has been different from mine. There are ways that we understand each other immediately. "Grieving is circular, not linear," I said to friends over brunch last weekend. "It comes around again and again." Bill looked up from his French toast.

"It's like Parcheesi," he said. "You keep being sent back to Start."

"You're right," I said. "That's a great metaphor."

I'm going to remember that, I thought. It *is* a great metaphor. But sometimes I feel that Bill gets back into the game with more gusto than I do. He maintains his passion in his work, and his involvement with his colleagues and friends and family, without slipping so easily into the undercurrent of sadness that I'm prone to. He has always been able to engage more fully in whatever he's doing than I, and to put everything else aside. I can't give up listening —not only for the sounds of others, but to the stirrings within myself.

And yet... I have learned to turn those stirrings into something of value. Putting words on the page absorbs and excites me. I wasn't a writer before Sean died, although I must have had a secret yearning to become one. I was a literature major in college, and I wrote papers that I knew were good, but they were always about other people's prose or poetry. I was a child who colored within the lines, and as I grew older I still couldn't take a chance on my own imagination.

Losing Sean ripped something open in me. It left me breathless and vulnerable, but with an unexpectedly tenacious will to survive. That night in Jackson Hole, after Ashley told us that Sean had been killed, I didn't sleep at all. I remember wondering at one point during those long wakeful hours if I cared whether I lived or died, and realizing immediately that I did care. Not just for Bill and our daughters, but for myself. I couldn't yet take in what had happened, but I knew that I didn't want a life that was stunted by Sean's death.

And so I struggled to reclaim my own energy and life force. When Sean died I was someone who was not clear what her passions were, but as my initial numbness waned, I knew that I had a passion to live. Each morning I felt as if I took deep gulps of air and began a run for my life. My determination to fight surprised me.

In one sense I was helpless. I had lost someone whom I loved without measure, and I could not bring him back. But what I could do was bear witness to my pain by recording it, and then by fashioning something new from the raw material of it. Writing became a way of not submitting, of becoming an actor in the drama of Sean's death by creating something from it.

When I write I suspend my feelings of emptiness and despair. In the act of creating I hold at bay loneliness, yearning, rage—even as I write about them. I may feel a sense of pleasure in what I'm making. When I stop, the terrible feelings don't rush back in for a while. I experience an illusion of resolution. An illusion, because the fact that Sean is dead, and that I long for him, will never go away.

A lot of my writing is about finding my way back to Sean, to holding him in whatever way I can. I'm stunned that five years have gone by since I've seen him, even though life with him seems so far away from today's life with our new family. And yet Sean pervades this life, our life with our grandchildren. We look for him in them, and already Will and Hunter look at photos of him and parrot his name.

Writing is Sean's legacy to me. He was a free spirit, who hungered for new experiences. I don't have him anymore to be my free spirit, but after he died I took a chance on writing. I discovered that his death had unleashed in me not only an unruly intensity of pain, but also a gift of expression.

I am not writing for him, though. I'm clear about that. "Sean would have wanted you to go on with your life." That phrase rings hollow to me. Sean would have wanted to go on with *his* life. And I have been left to go on with mine in the way that *I* choose.

In the face of loss there's an urgency not only to pre-serve, but to create. A long submerged passion for words and their rhythm has awakened in me since Sean died. When I write I draw on a part of myself that is lively and excited, powerful and even joyous. At times I've felt guilty about gaining something for myself from Sean's death. I have come to believe, though, that something must hap-pen—either submission or creation. It's not possible to remain unchanged by a loss of this magnitude.

WHEN I WALK into my study, I'm reminded of Sean. The glass table on which my computer sits is placed against the wall where Sean's bed once was, the bed that now belongs to Will. The carpet on the floor is badly stained by the puppy that Sean begged for, and promised to walk, but didn't. The blue paint on the woodwork, the handiwork of Bill and the two Seans, is chipped. On one window is a sticker with the Nyack Public Schools logo. From another I can look northward and see the sailboats moored at the Nyack Boat Club, where Sean learned to sail. It is October, and the leaves are turning, and soon the boats will be brought in for the winter.

This room is now mine. The deep cherry wood of the early Victorian desk that my mother bought me when I was a child gives it warmth. The desk's cubbyholes are stuffed with receipts and bank statements, and it is topped with family pictures. On the south wall a cheap mahogany bookcase overflows with too many books. A Hepplewhite chair upholstered in faded pink, which belonged to my parents, is piled with folders. They don't quite hide the needlepoint pillow with an intricate pink and green floral pattern that Bill's mother made for me.

I've been thinking lately about replacing the carpet, perhaps with the antique Oriental that Bill brought me from Turkey. Its colors are blue, so dark it is almost black, and a deep gold that glows in sunlight. I'd like to repaint the woodwork a pale ivory that would complement soft yellow walls, and invest in a good bookcase. It would be fun to look around for artwork, and a plush armchair for reading. Perhaps I'll spend the winter playing with ideas and redecorate in the spring.

I am content here. Writing these words astonishes me. I didn't know if I could ever be content again.

Printed in the United States
50862LVS00003B/175-177

9 780977 620753